Publication History

First edition, November 2023

Second edition, February 2024 (Wrexham)

Third edition, April 2024 (Southampton)

Praise for the international seller[1] "92"

"It's not Bad" – Adam (Fulham)

"It's a good bed time book…" – Dave (Stoke)

"Book is enjoyable" – Joe (Wimbledon)

"I like it a lot" – Tony (Chelsea)

"Curmudgeonly Yorkshire no nonsense scepticism" – Mike (Man U)

---

[1] Thanks Klaas!

About The Author

Duncan started life in Yeadon, a market town close to both Bradford and Leeds. The easy route could have been to follow Leeds. But with a Dad from London who was a Chelsea fan and hated "Dirty Leeds" this was going to be a challenge. Duncan likes to eat. In fact, the Bradford allegiance came from his Grandad. Yeadon born and bred, grandad George was born in 1904, so as a 7 year old he saw Bradford City win the FA Cup and finish 5th in the league. At this point Leeds Utd didn't even exist. Grandad George was a Bradford fan so of course Bradford it was.

Duncan went to school at Woodhouse Grove, which is where Bradford now train. He was in the school first team for football at the age of 9 and was once trained by a Bradford City player but history has forgotten which one! (1973/74 season if anyone remembers). "Duncan is turning out to be a good full back, he tackles hard and plays well" reads the school report. On moving up to big school it was rugby only. No football. This has left Duncan with a deep seated dislike of all things rugby. Duncan has not lived in the Bradford area since he was 18 but returns regularly for the football, beers and curry.

Disclaimer from the Author

This book is built on facts, opinions and memories.

The facts, I have done my best to research, let me know if you find an error.

The opinions are my own, feel free to disagree. That is the point.

The memories. I know from writing this book, memories can play you false. This is how I remember it all. But then I still swear I remember Chris Waddle scoring from the half way line at Goodison.

Introduction

It's an unusual hobby being a football fan. Tell someone who shares your passion that you love fly-fishing or macramé or wargaming and you have a friend for life. Tell a football fan who your team is and unless you strike the jackpot you will invariably encounter premier league snobbery, disinterest or worse, open enmity, probably to some perceived crime committed in the late 60's, or last weekend, or anywhere in between. "You stole our goalkeeper/manager/cleaner. Etc." It's hard to engender genuine interest, but for those of us who drive the motorway network or ride the rail system (if it's working) to the away games we can share a common bond of excitement in the away fan experience. Well, at least at the other 90 grounds. Probably.

Before I go any further, a couple of points to clarify. Firstly, I am not a member of the 92 club. I wouldn't want to be. Who wants to be a member of a club they can get into? This is a personal journey, and I don't see the need to prove my attendance, nor do I agree with their rule that you have to have been to the current ground. I have been to around 120 grounds, but for me it is about the clubs not the grounds. Secondly, this book is not about the team I support, or the team you support, it is about going to away games. There will be moaning Bradford fans reading this book getting all wound up by me calling my team Bradford all the time when really I should call them City. For it is written (nowhere in particular) Bradford are Park Avenue! My club is Bradford City. You see how easy it is to fall out in a shared hobby. But for the fans reading this book who are not Bradford fans "City" would just be confusing. So Bradford it is.

This book starts on Tuesday February 19th, 1974, or possibly on Wednesday 7th March 1984. Or in fact, according to my spreadsheet, it starts on 29th December 1984. Let me explain.

My first taste of football came about totally out of the blue thanks to the 1970's miners' strike. The local "big" team Leeds United (or Scum as they are affectionately referred to by most Bradford fans, and indeed most other teams) were due to play an unfancied lower league Bristol City in an FA Cup replay. My neighbours had tickets, but thanks to Government regulations, brought in to reduce electricity use due to the ongoing strike all but 'essential' industries switched to a three-day week, power guzzling floodlights could not be switched on, so, as a replay, the game had to be played in daylight during a working day. Homes were regularly hit by power cuts. I loved the power cuts. I had a Subbuteo set with battery operated floodlights. When a power cut hit I could simulate a proper magical night under the lights. I had a Bradford team, a Leeds team, a Chelsea team (my Dad's team) and a Liverpool team. So I could do semi-finals as well.

Back to the football, A midweek 2pm kick-off time, no one could attend except for me aged 8 and my Grandad (retired), so off we went. At 8 years old my memories are scant. I remember a huge sea of humanity washing up and down the terraces, I couldn't believe people weren't being trampled to death and was grateful (for once) to be sat, away from the action and just soak up the tremendous noise of the day. Incredibly, even better for my day, Leeds lost 1-0, a shock result which actually made the front page of the newspapers. I was hooked.

I would have gone every week, but my Dad refused. "Bloody hooligans, we should set the dogs on the lot of them" was all I got if I ever suggested we went. So that was that, my teenage years arrived, I discovered beer, girls and motorbikes and football disappeared into the background.

Then in 1984 I found myself at Liverpool University on a mundane Wednesday in March and my mate Alan said, "Liverpool are playing Benfica in the European Cup quarter final tonight – shall we go?" – Really – will we get in?– yeah pay on the gate – is it expensive - £2 (£2!), right I'm in. So off we went.

This time as an 18 year old, no seat for me, standing on the kop and to see a team I liked, playing at the top of their game.

Again, the wall of noise was electric, the huge surges up and down across the kop. Feeling slightly like intruders we stood to the side near the bottom and drank it all in. A man near us had "smuggled" his 2 month old son in under his coat. And when in the 46th minute Kenny Dalglish was introduced, coming back from injury, he waved his son aloft screaming "Look at that son, Kenny Dalglish, the greatest player in the world, you won't see a player like that again". Liverpool won 1-0, Ian Rush scoring with a header in front of the kop. Liverpool went on to win the European Cup in Rome with the famous Grobbelaar wobbly legs penalty shoot-out, that season. Again, I was hooked and this time it stuck. I bought a season ticket (£42) and was lucky enough to see two of the best Liverpool teams there have ever been during my time living in Liverpool in the 80's. First Dalglish and Rush, with Lawrenson and Hansen at the back and in the later 80's Barnes, Beardsley and Aldridge. But I always felt an interloper. This was a great team but it wasn't my team.

I found my team on 29th December 1984 at Valley Parade. My local team, a pretty average (poor, really) team, but a team I felt part of, not an interested observer, with a right to be there. This book tells the story of my journey to watch Bradford at all 92 football grounds. A journey which is not entirely complete, despite 120 or so grounds to date. And when you think about it, a journey which can never be complete. Solihull Moors next season?

In defining my personal 92 I have my own idiosyncratic rules, not the 92 club rules. These are my rules. If I have seen a club play at home, I have seen that club, better if I have seen them play Bradford. The up to date spreadsheet of progress is in the appendix.

Finally, I appreciate there will be a temptation to skip straight to your club. A word of warning. Memories fade. Some clubs get their own chapter, some clubs only a paragraph. Special apologies to Burnley fans, I visited Turf Moor (apparently) on 15th January 1994 – I have no recollection of this game whatsoever! Even the programmes I bought in the early years don't always help. The Burnley programme for that day assures me that Kevin Sheedy was playing in midfield. Whilst he would have been more than welcome, my memory and Wikipedia confirm that unfortunately, Kevin never came to Bradford.

Try to enjoy the ride as an away fan. On an away day a win is always an unexpected bonus.

I am sure you will find mistakes in this book (please tell me!). I have probably been to over a thousand games so I am sure I have forgotten loads. With the wonders of modern on line publishing I will update my book regularly as I visit new grounds.

THE KLAAS YEARS

Section 1 – The Klaas Years 1984 - 1993

I am indebted to Klaas, or possibly I should blame him? For starting me on the road to the Bradford 92. Nicolaas Smeele, as Bradfordian as the next man, but with Dutch parents, hence the unusual name, Klaas (for short).

My early years of chasing the 92 were often along a familiar pattern. Living away from Bradford it would be a quick phone call, "Bradford are away at Crewe, Port Vale etc tonight – see you behind the goal." No internet, no tickets, no sat nav, pay on the gate and no worries that it might sell out. Klaas now lives in New Zealand, so the Klaas years are definitely over, but he has been known to pop over for the occasional game, once a decade…

It was Klaas who introduced me to the idea of a pint before the game. A whole raft of home pubs that have now passed into history. The Carlton Hotel, The Oakleigh, The Spotted House and Haigys, the exterior of the pub beautifully painted in claret and amber. Now all gone. I'm sure you have the same for your team.

The latest to fall being The Sparrow, an excellent pub, friendly to both home and away fans and handy for the ground but now sadly boarded up and awaiting its fate. We move on and you will currently find me in the Boar and Fable or The Exchange, up to 30 minutes before the game, But I get ahead of myself.

Bradford (City)

This book is about the away ground experience, so there is an element of guesswork to my views on this ground as I have only been as a home fan. Let us start at the very beginning.

Assuming your idea of a good day out was not a punch up, in 1984 Bradford was not a great away day. My mate Mark (a Derby fan with a Derby accent) was up visiting for Xmas, so

Klaas, Mark and I caught the train the short ride from Bingley into Bradford for the Xmas game, Bradford vs Bolton. Accents were very important in the 80's at football matches. Klaas being of Dutch forebears actually had a cracking Braford accent, certainly compared to the rest of us. Mark as mentioned had a Derby accent, and though this was definitively not a Bolton accent "We hate Derby and we hate Derby" at the time, so that was not a good choice. Finally there's me. I have a non-descript, vaguely northern (to southerners) vaguely posh (to Bradfordians) accent, I think. I was once on a night out with Klaas in Bradford and we got talking to some girls, as you do. They were quite intrigued. "You tork ded funneh" they said to me. You get the point.

Klaas, being an old hand at this, took the lead as we made the mile walk from Forster square along Manningham Lane to Valley Parade. I think we got asked the time 3 times by youths hanging out in doorways. Three times Klaas took the lead and responded. They were looking for a fight with Boltonians, but Derby would probably have done. I'm not sure what they would have made of me.

Into the ground and it was no better. For some unknown reason, some genius had decided that it was a good idea to split the kop in two. A large part for the home fans and a smaller part for the away fans. Add to this the fact that the kop was visibly crumbling and you had a recipe for a good rubble throwing party. Ridiculous. Anyhow, we survived, and the ground did not last much longer. I will not cover that here other than to say I was not there on the day of the fire so I have nothing to add other than my sadness. RIP 56.

The man on the roof. If you went to valley parade in the 80's or early 90's you would have seen the man on the roof. There are a lot of grounds around the country where it is easy to kick the ball clear over the stand. But valley parade is the only ground where I have seen a man standing on the roof of the offending small stand. The thing is, no one seems to know why he was there. He certainly wasn't trying to stop the ball. Valley parade is built into a steep hillside so if he had fallen off attempting to stop the ball he would have had quite a steep drop. He also didn't seem to be directing the ball recovery operation. I'm afraid to say I always cheered when the ball headed his way and he always got out of the way. I remember Steve Staunton kicking it his way with his first kick of the ball at valley parade. Steve got better. I have googled it but I can't find any hard evidence of who the man on the roof was or why he was there. I have hearsay that he was a milkman named Derek from Shipley. That sounds right?

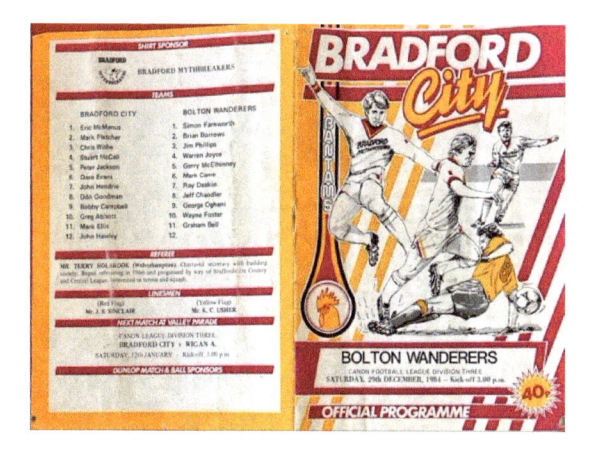

In its later years the stand roof was also used as a rather precarious looking TV gantry. Pity the guys who worked there on a cold Tuesday night. The stand was replaced and reopened in 1996. The steel from the old stand was sold to Barrow who intended to use it for their ground. But during their insolvency the steel "apparently disappeared".

Today, I hope, the experience of the away fan is vastly improved. Apart from on the busiest of days or with fans from teams with a troublesome reputation the away fans are welcomed into the pubs and it's all very jolly. Let me personally recommend The Corn Dolly, or the Exchange. If, however you support a "big" team or a "bad" team you may well have to make do with the Bradford Arms on Manningham Lane, half way from the station to the ground. I have never been in but it looks awful. I would say one thing in its defence. On a busy away day the away fans do seem to generate a cracking atmosphere in there.

Anyway, I hope I am not biased when I suggest that today, Bradford is in the top 10 for cracking away days, good pubs, good pies, easy to park. Just don't get a time machine and go back to 1984.

Huddersfield

Huddersfield is the obvious place to start for a Bradford away game and indeed you would have found Klaas and I on the uncovered terrace in September 1985. I have been to Huddersfield more times than I care to remember. Not least because Bradford played some home games there whilst rebuilding after the fire. It was the early days for me so I had no idea what to expect as an away fan, and life in the 80's indeed often didn't provide much. Not only an open air terrace but also an open air toilet, the urinal being a wall with a ceramic gutter at the bottom. I was happy and wanted more.

Huddersfield, probably quite rightly, weren't happy and wanted more for themselves than an al-fresco toilet solution and they were an early mover in the wave of new ground building. So the late 90's saw me back for a new ground.

There is of course a rivalry between the two clubs, being so close by. But I have never been part of it. In the 90's when chat rooms were getting started we began arranging friendlies with the rival fans for a game of football before the game. 11 a side and surprisingly good fun and very polite and well behaved. I've seen much worse behaviour most weeks at my sons U 11 games (he referees now). In the last game I played at Huddersfield I even scored a goal in the last minute. A consolation as we lost 4-3. A decent bunch of lads from a decent town with some very acceptable pubs. I would also say that of all the "new" grounds that I've visited, this is probably one of the best. Decent architecture, decent parking and pubs within walking distance. Take note Stoke City, Derby County, Walsall etc.

It's been over 20 years now since I've been to Huddersfield for a match. I'm guessing it wouldn't be pay on the gate any more.

Reading

Reading was my first experience of travelling to an away game on my own, and how naïve I was. At the time I was living in Liverpool doing a PhD which involved regular trips to the Atomic Energy Authority in Harwell, just south of Oxford and hence not too far from Reading. Remember the ill-fated attempt to merge Oxford and Reading to be the "Thames Valley Royals"? Not a popular memory for the Reading or Oxford fans!

It didn't escape my notice that Reading was just a couple of train stops down the line and as an impoverished student, anything for free travel...By "uncanny" chance I found myself needing a visit to Harwell the day before Bradford were due to play Reading, so the trip was on. But it's fair to say I hadn't entirely thought this through. My usual youthful "It'll be reet" approach which has now sadly been replaced by my middle aged approach of – "Right, let's think about all the things that could go wrong". It does usually turn out OK.

So, with my happy go lucky approach I find myself stood outside Elm Park at about 1.30 on Saturday 11th April 1987. Overnight bag in hand. Waiting to get into the away terrace. "What you got there then" asks the steward – not unreasonably. At this point my carefree attitudes begins to evaporate, quite quickly. "Ah, just my overnight things plus my sample pots from my experiments at the Atomic Energy Authority" – ho hum. "They're not radioactive are they" gulps the steward who probably hasn't come across this before. "No, but they are in sealed metal vacuum pots (ideal missiles?), oh and there are a few scalpels in there as well". This is not sounding good is it? I had decided to come clean and was beginning to think that at best I was not seeing the game. "OK, well take them to the main reception and collect them after the game" was the entirely unexpected and reasonable response – Cheers Reading! And they certainly didn't think about charging me for the service. Take note Tottenham Hotspur.

Elm Park, as was, was seemingly built as a natural wind tunnel. And there was a pretty fierce wind in just the right direction that day. City were in the relegation mix and desperate to avoid a return to the third tier. Reading were out of the mire but no great shakes that season, so this was an opportunity, we needed something. Batten down the hatches in the first half playing into the wind and see if we get to half time still in touch. We made it through to half time and sure enough the second half was a "breeze" – sorry!. John Hendrie, twinkle toes himself, conjured the only goal of the game and we were out of the relegation zone. But with a lot of work to do for safety. I needn't have worried as we won 5 of our next 6 games and were well out of trouble by the final day. Back to reception to collect my bag and the job was a good un. Back home in Liverpool well before last orders.

I have since been back to Reading for their new ground, the Madejski stadium, but it's a soulless out of town aberration and really not for me. Such a shame. I loved Elm Park.

Further memories for the Madejski. In the early years of Tony (section 3) Bradford were on an unfeasible FA cup run and despite being third tier, having dispatched premier league Chelsea and Sunderland, were one win away from an FA Cup semi-final trip to Wembley. Tony moaned and pestered me to get a ticket and eventually, the day before, I relented and at the last minute ordered a ticket to be picked up from the supporters coach at the ground. Tony and I wouldn't be sat (stood!) together but we would share the journey down. Then Pat (see section 2) rang to say his brother Eddie had a ticket for the directors lounge (well, how could I refuse!). Now I had two tickets but I knew which I was using! Tony was driving, so an extra drink for me!. I got into the Executive suite, had a quick drink, and on the toilet trip was stood next to Mark Lawn, our owner (at the time, how I wish he still was) and all round jolly chap. I accosted him with the warmth that alcohol provides and he did his best considering he had no idea who I was. He didn't seem to fancy our chances much. Anyway, back to the prawn sandwiches. But my phone rang. "Duncan, you have to leave now, my mate has decided to come to the game and he's wondering where his ticket is!". No bother, I will go collect my other ticket. So back outside I now discover the supporters coach is late – so no second ticket. The coach eventually arrives 15 minutes after kick off and I make my way into the ground just in time to see Reading score. We lose 3-0. And the Reading fans send us home with a few choruses of "You've come a long way for nothing". I knew I didn't like new grounds.

Derby County

In the relegation battle of 86/87 Bradford put in a tremendous end of season show to win 7 games out of 8. The one blemish to that was Derby, who to be fair, were top. And of course I was at this game. 20th April 1987. At the time there was a lot of bad feeling amongst Bradford fans about the way Derby had "stolen" Roy McFarland away from us. I didn't really feel this way, possibly because the bad blood was before I started watching in earnest. McFarland won us promotion in 81/82 from the fourth tier – where I had grown used to us residing. Oh for a McFarland today! McFarland then left to join Derby in let's say somewhat controversial circumstances and Derby eventually had to pay a hefty fine. No matter, Bradford continued to improve on the so-called wave of "Bantam Progressivism" without him, but it certainly made for a great atmosphere. The Bradford fans spent pretty much the entire game singing. "McBastard", "Bahhhh" and "Sheep Shaggers" springing to mind as the chants I remember. My mate Mark the Derby fan was with me, but he doesn't take these things to heart. In fact, he's one of these strange football fans who supports all the local clubs. Anything East Midlands is fine by him. This is not my way at all !

Derby, of course, won 1-0 with Mark Lillis scoring the only goal. As a footnote to the game, the program listed nationalities that day and I remember noticing that of Derby's 11, 10 were English, The odd one out being Geraint Williams, no prizes for guessing his birth place. How the game has changed.

I have since been back to the new ground twice. Pride Park, a soulless out of town aberration complete with the obligatory Subway and TGI Fridays. Such a shame. I loved the baseball park. Sometimes there was even grass on the pitch. Not good enough.

The second time I went with a Derby fan to see if local knowledge could improve the experience. Beers at the Smithfield, a proper old fashioned working mans pub with 8 real ales and a 20 minute walk to the ground along the river and past a surprisingly noisy riparian bird population. Derby now have "safe standing". It's awful. A pale anodised travesty of the former glory of standing on an open terrace and swaying with the mass. You now get an allocated seat and a bar in front of you. At least you don't have an argument about whether its ok to stand, but other than that it's just sad. The worlds most passionate bradford fan, Charlie sat down!

The game itself felt like a throwback to the 90's. An EFL Trophy game, so a sparse crowd. 700 Bradford fans in good voice and amongst a 1,000 or so from Derby a hard core of around 50 (mostly kids) prepared to chant back at the top of the Derby mainstand. Amongst the Derby mob was a rotund older man, Cue the chants "Do do do, fatty in an Umbro" and other less printable lyrics. "Fatty" couldn't resist taking his top off to show off his prize belly. Happy days. Soon after he was escorted from the stands to more hilarity. I couldn't see why.

Shrewsbury

"Here comes another winter of long shadows and high hopes" sang The The in "Heartland" in the mid 80's and it certainly felt that way in 1987. Without giving the game away, this is the "nearly" season for Bradford and the next line of the song is, "Here comes another winter, waiting for utopia, waiting for hell to freeze over". Anyway, back in September 1987 optimism was high in Bradford.

As you can see from the matchday programme I used to keep a track of the players and the scores. Interesting art work from the Shrews?

We had carried our late season form straight into the new season and we were top!, Indeed by October we would find ourselves 6 points clear. We travelled down from Liverpool by train, full of hope and happy in the last rays of the early Autumn sunshine. The town itself was and still is gorgeous. To a lad raised in Bradford and living in Liverpool it was like arriving in paradise. And the pubs, such a treat. This was back in the days when most pubs were tied houses serving dull beers from the large brewers and few offered much to get excited about back in Liverpool. But the Shrewsbury pubs were enough to make you want to stay for a holiday. One of the pubs we went to was the "Three Fishes" on Fish Street of course. This oasis was a smoke free zone back in the 90's. What an incredible experience to have a couple of pints of Landlord and not smell of fags afterwards. I've checked and it's still in the Beer Guide today.

The ground itself was a treasure too. A short walk from the city centre and for the finishing touch, with a man in a coracle on the river in case the ball got hoofed in that direction. The local papers were excited about the prospect of that great double act, McCall and Hendrie being in town today, but in truth, Shrewsbury raised their game that day and gave at least as good as they got. Heading into injury time the Shrews were 2-1 up. Cue a delightful ball into the box and up pops sticks himself Ian Ormondroyd to slam home an unstoppable header. Scenes, if it hadn't been for the anti-hooligan railings I'm sure Ian would have jumped into the crowd to celebrate. I think this was my first experience of that greatest of football joys, the last minute goal. Surely the best feeling? We all left happy that day.

I have been back a number of times to Shrewsbury and the town remains lovely. In the 90's I went twice more, once on my own and once with Pat. This fixture reliably adds another layer of memory each time. In November 94 I visited on my own. Bradford won 2-1 but the game is memorable for the Shrewsbury goal. Get your hands on the VHS goals of the season highlights for Bradford City that season and you can clearly see me in the away end as Shrewsbury score. As the Shrews go through the usual celebration antics I can be seen feigning complete disinterest and checking the change in my pocket. Always a highlight to get on the telly. I also had a rather unwise goatee beard, that didn't last long.

The following season a very uneventful 1-1 draw had drawn to a close and we were driving home on the dual carriageway heading towards the M6. I was driving a company hire car I had managed to wangle to provide free transport, it's fair to say I was travelling at a significant speed as usual in the last of these halcyon pre speed trap years, when suddenly a car beamed down in front of us apparently from Planet Zanussi. I slammed on my brakes and got my first real, heat of the moment sense of just how good these new ABS brakes can be in a crisis. We somehow contrived not to slam into the back of the car that had appeared in the outside lane from nowhere and after a few mutual exchanges of gesticulations we carried on home. No harm done, although I swear I must have flat spotted the discs and/or the tyres. Still the hire car company seemed happy.

That was the lovely old ground, but what have they done with the new ground? They say you can tell the difference between a pub and a bar, because if you take all the furniture and beer out of a pub, it still looks like a pub, whereas a bar looks like a room. For me these new grounds are the same, football equivalents of bars not pubs. But I'm not even sure who they are for. The parking isn't easier (apart from at Stevenage), there are usually no decent pubs and the train station is usually miles away. When you go to a football match you should feel like you are going to a football match, not to IKEA.!

I have been to the Montgomery Waters (really is that what it's called?) stadium, but it's a soulless out of town aberration and not for me. There are high quality new stadia being built, but they seem to predominantly be in London. I do have some hopes for the Everton ground. Maybe Bradford can get into the championship in a few years time and find out..

Ticking Off the Grounds

By now I had developed a real taste for new grounds and to some extent I didn't care who was playing – it was all fun to me. Here's a sample:

West Ham – 20th May 1985. I really should be studying for my second year exams in Liverpool but Liverpool FC are doing a £1 return football special to the Boleyn Ground for a totally pointless end of season game. Who could resist? Me and Mark pop on the train and immediately wonder where everybody is. There can't have been more than 30 of us on the train down to London. Could it be a bit lonely in the away end? By some magic of train routing the train drops us within a short walk to the ground and we are quickly ushered from the station into a full on police cordoned escort of away fans, straight into the ground. Suddenly there are thousands of Liverpool fans, all with London accents! Liverpool spank West Ham and there's a pitch invasion of unhappy Hammers at the end. Come on lads it's really not that important is it?

I still haven't seen Bradford at West Ham, though I have walked past the new stadium. That's one for a cup game I think.

Blackpool – My girlfriend at the time was from Blackpool, and although not a Blackpool fan herself it would have been rude not to take a look, or two. In the end I went twice, once to stand on the decaying and unpopulated terracing and marvel that Stanley Matthews had once played here. Once in the posh seats (I can't remember how that happened – maybe her Dad paid?) to check on our old Bradford hero Bobby Campbell, seeing out his last playing days for Wigan Athletic.

Wrexham – It's the 19th April 1988. I still can't drive a car but I have a mate who can. And he's a Kidderminster Harriers fan. It turns out that through some interesting interpretation of geography Kidderminster are playing at Wrexham in the Welsh Cup semifinal. Well, what are we waiting for. We all sing the "Where the hell are you from" (We're from Kidderminster, lovely Kidderminster) song and I try to do a Brummie accent.

In my youthful confidence I know I will be back to all these three clubs at some point, I have no doubt.

As it turns out, the first revisit was Wrexham in 2024, I am replete with loyalty points so I didn't need to worry about getting a ticket for the sold out away end. You can read the results at the end of the book.

Barnsley, Get used to losing.

For pretty much every fan, an away day trip does not start with an overwhelming feeling of confidence that you will win. You might win, but you are more likely to lose. Travel with an "anything is a bonus" mentality and away support becomes a way of life. It's possible to put up with the disappointments because you feel like an explorer. Even in a season when you think you will get promoted, you seem to mostly lose. That takes us to Barnsley.

Barnsley. I know people who have never left Bradford, You probably know people like this from your area too. Its surprisingly common. A fan did confide in me that the furthest away from Bradford he had ever been was Barnsley (It is 30 miles away from Bradford), on the supporters coach, but we lost so he wouldn't be doing that again. When I first visited Barnsley it had a huge capacity, something like 38,000. And all but 500 of it terracing. There were tales of hardened away fans buying season tickets just to guarantee a seat on their club's visit. It's all seater today of course and I have been back many times. But I don't think we have ever won. My first visit was in the nearly season. On paper we were much better than mid table Barnsley. We lost 3-0. It's that type of place.

Tony and I went back for the last time to date in January 2019. We were awful and heading for relegation. You could tell the day was not going to go well. The pub we had carefully researched was full and wouldn't let us in. We ended up in a sensationally dire working mens club. Up there in the top 3 away day worst pubs I have been in. And we lost 3-0 again. Maybe one day we will win.

Leeds

It's difficult to not go off on one about Leeds, but what's the point. They do seem capable of regularly shooting themselves in the foot just when they look to have turned a corner. So all the best to our near neighbours. Keep on shooting. I have a lot of good friends who are Leeds fans, but they do seem to attract a greater share of "colourful" fans than most clubs. These days everything seems relatively calm but it was vicious in the 80's.

I've never been able to sing. I think I'm tone deaf and dumb. Of course this doesn't stop me from singing. Klaas and I were singing our hearts out as usual in the away end at Elland Road. The thing with away games is you are stood next to someone who is not used to you. So this guy turns round and says "you two were never in the choir" – How rude!. But entirely accurate.

Of course we lost to Leeds at Elland Road in the nearly season. That was to be expected. The fun part was actually after the final whistle. For some reason we had persuaded Klaas' brother Joost to come. He really doesn't get football. But he survived the 90 minutes ok. The trouble started as we left the ground. Somehow we got split up. We looked for him but couldn't find him and eventually decided he knew where we had parked. So Klaas and I made our way to the car park. In those days, the car park was still one of those vast areas of land that looks like it hasn't been touched since the Germans stopped bombing. You don't get many of those any more. We waited and waited and waited. Eventually the car park was empty so we went home. Two and a half hours later Joost turned up. He'd had quite a walk, apparently ending up on the motorway at one point. It's ok Joost – we won't make you come again.

Birmingham City

My first visit to St Andrews was on 5th March 1988 for a second tier game. Jasper Carrot is a well-known celebrity fan at Birmingham and he used to tell a joke. "I was at St Andrews on Saturday, I turned round to the chap next to me" – At this point he dramatically cups his hands to his mouth and bellows "nice and quiet here today!". It's a big ground and the crowd that day was 8,000 so it certainly seemed quite sparse. Getting towards the business end of the season, Bradford are 5th and looking like a decent play-off bet. So there's a decent level of expectation in the away end. There's a fair amount of disgruntlement from the home fans at their poor performance. They should worry. In three years I will be back, for a third tier game after we have both been relegated. Things can always get worse.

It's funny how the memories of the travel (for me) are often sharper than the memories of the game. I was still carless at the time so it's a train direct from Liverpool, followed by a horrible half hour walk to the ground. Let's be honest that walk hasn't improved? Same walk back, but at least I know there's a nice pub inside New Street station for a bit of after match therapy. I start up a conversation with some Boro fans who have been to Villa, while we drink our beers and wait for the train. They all look a bit shocked, should we be talking to each other or fighting (The 80's). Some things have improved since the 80's at least.

Here's a list of things that are better today than in the 80's: - Less fighting, better pitches, (hence?) better football in general, the pubs (mostly)

Here's a list of things that are worse: - Sky TV kick off times, No standing, Ticket prices, Wembley FA Cup semi-finals, the atmosphere, harder to get a ticket, rolling around in feigned agony, the refereeing?

I'm not sure about the refereeing. But having refereed and umpired myself I know that I have always given an honest decision and no doubt some of these were wrong. In the 80's a "bad" decision just served to improve the atmosphere, even if you were lucky enough to get a TV replay (eventually) it was often too grainy to be clear. Now everything is analysed in minute Ultra High Definition detail. I don't think it helps. VAR should be for "clear and obvious errors" only. If it takes 2 minutes (or more) or you have to draw lines, stick with the on-field decision. The game should be for the crowd, we shouldn't be waiting around to see if we can cheer or not.

Fortunately Bradford are a long way away from VAR concerns. We do still get a lot of bad decisions though... (as says every fan of every team?).

Aston Villa

The "nearly season" 1987/88 is drawing to its conclusion. Stuart McCall and John Hendie, the gargantuan twin pillars of what remains one of the best teams and best league performances of a Bradford City team in my lifetime trying their best to drag an otherwise competent but average squad into the top flight . The scene is set with Bradford lying third in the Division 2 table (Championship if you will). Two teams go up, Millwall are top on 76 points, Villa second on 74 and Bradford third also on 74 but with a game in hand. For the only time in my football watching career I take the Bradford supporters coach along with Klaas.

Back then Villa were managed by Graham Taylor (do I not like that) and had Martin Keown, Tony Daley and from midfield David Platt boasting 25 goals so far this season. It was never going to be easy.

The game finished 1-0 to Villa with David Platt (of course) scoring the winning goal. As the City players trudged off the pitch our defender, Lee Sinnott grabbed the ball, hid it under his shirt and threw it into the away supporters end, thus ensuring a mad scramble. The following day I swear there were 6 separate balls all advertised in the local newspaper, the Telegraph & Argus, all claiming to be the original match ball!

What a ground this used to be with the terraced Holte end. Sadly demolished in 1994 and now all seating as can be seen in my photo below (taken at a work conference in 2017). The atmosphere used to be electric and every inch suited its status as a regular host of FA Cup semi-finals. Please bring these games back where they belong. Yes, use Wembley for a London derby, but for Arsenal vs Liverpool (say), this is where the game should be.

I did in fact watch a cup replay at Villa Park.

Imagine the following series of events happening now:

Liverpool were drawn to play Arsenal in the third round of the League Cup at Anfield. Third round, would either team even be in it by then?

The game was drawn and so replayed at Highbury one week (!) later. If this was today there would be no replay and straight to penalties after 90 minutes. A crowd of over 54,000 watched the replay with a further 6,000 locked out. There are photos in The Guardian of fans sat on the Highbury roof watching the game – which also ended as a draw. Afterwards Kenny Dalglish expressed his relief that the game would not be settled on penalties as he felt this would have devalued the competition!

The tie went to a second replay at Villa Park on 23rd November 1988 and I attended (again in the away end) to see Liverpool finally win 2-1. Incredibly, the programme for the second replay records that if scores are level after 90 minutes there will be 30 minutes of extra time. If scores are still level there would have been another replay!

The league cup has fallen a long way.

Sheffield Wednesday

29th March 1986. I am home in Bradford with my mate Klaas and its 1.30 pm. We are young and bored, what shall we do. I know, Liverpool are at Sheffield Wednesday – lets go. So off we speed at a rate that I would describe as "pre speed cameras" and arrive at Hillsboro at approx. 2.50 pm. It's absolutely heaving! I really do need to start thinking things through? I am not much of a runner but off we set sprinting to the ground and then around the ground as turnstiles are locked. Eventually we find one turnstile still open. We are on to the massive seething terraces that used to be the Wednesday home end. The game is an utterly unmemorable 0-0 draw. The worst result Liverpool will record in their run in as they cruise to the league title, winning something like 7 of their last 8. But what an atmosphere. By the way, this was one month before the last ever game on the uncovered kop at Hillsborough. 3rd May 1986 vs Ipswich Town, and so the gentrification begins!

We were back home in Bingley for beers in plenty of time for tea before the standard meet of 8-30 in The Ferrands Arms for beers. And that's really where Hillsborough should have ended for me, but..

9th April 1988. Liverpool are due to play Forest at Hillsborough in the FA Cup Semi Final. I have a season ticket at Liverpool (I'm living in Liverpool – a season ticket is £46 that season and Liverpool are a joy to watch in 1988 – why wouldn't you?). It's easy to get a ticket and the supporters coach is a £1. Great day out – or so I thought.

We arrived at the ground around 2 pm – half the occupants went off to find a pub and we went straight into the ground. Liverpool had been given the Leppings lane away end. My first trip to this ground so as usual you go through the turnstile – find yourself in a non-descript concrete area and head for the view of the pitch. Nothing unusual there, but this is a massive mistake as it turns out. For some unknown reason, and I have never seen this anywhere else, the designers have seen fit to put fences running up the terraces as well as barriers at the front. This means if you are in the middle "pen" you cannot spread out. An absolutely ridiculous design flaw. Bear in mind this was only 2 pm and even an hour before kick off we couldn't breathe it was so packed. "Sod this" I said and we fought our way out thankfully and managed to find the side terraces. Somehow the game went off without incident but I was livid about the design. When Liverpool drew exactly the same fixture the next year I refused to go and passed my ticket on to a friend – I am so sorry Mark (Not Derby Mark). I know Mark and Kim both had some awful experiences that day but at least they were forearmed so stood at the side. One of my fellow students was not so lucky and is now on the memorial plaque. RIP.

Which brings us to the Hillsborough report and the subsequent legislation requiring all seater stadia. We all know a lot of mistakes were made before, during and after the fateful day. All seater stadia was clearly not the worst decision or mistake, but it was so unnecessary. We were probably trending in the direction of more seating anyway with the gentrification of football in the 90's, but it seemed to me that this report was not written by the fans. Anyone who has stood on the terraces at a packed, Anfield, Elland Road, Stretford end, Holte end etc and sung as one with 10,000 or more voices the anthem of the club, will know, you get the hairs rising. I've set off the goose bumps in myself just thinking about it. It is a unique experience. It has now gone. I've been back to these grounds, they are a pale shade of yesteryear.

Maybe it was going anyway but it didn't need to be axed so suddenly. It's happened to pop concerts too now. It used to be cheap to buy a ticket to see your favourite band – you could force yourself to the front of the stage and jump up and down in a lather of sweat for a happy hour or so. Now chances are that same band want to charge you getting on for £200 to sit with 15,000 people in an anodyne crowd where you need binoculars to see the stage. I'd rather stay at home and listen to spotify.

The simple fact is some fans want to stand. The worst impact of all seater stadia has been the mixing of those who want to stand with those who want to sit. You've not been to an away game if you haven't had (or at least heard) the following conversation. "You're not going to stand all game are you?" – "Yes, of course" "Well I've paid for a seat" – "Well I can't pay to stand but I want to" And on and on. I would say I now stand at every away game that is more than 80% full (when it is less full the stewards get you to sit down). What is the point.

Scunthorpe

It is the 22nd November 1988. I am enjoying the newfound freedom of having passed my car test and having my own car. I'm living in Liverpool but when Klaas suggests a quick coast to coast to meet up behind the goal at Scunthorpe I can't resist. It's a Littlewoods Cup third round replay. Second tier Bradford (although heading downwards) have failed to see off fourth tier (although in 4th spot) Scunthorpe at home and so will have to do it the hard way.

Klaas has arranged to meet up with his mate Will. I don't really know why, as Will does not have the slightest interest in football. If there was a competition to sum up Will in one word I would go for "steady". He likes a beer for instance, but he drinks slowly. But then he never stops. I will down the first one quite quickly, then slow down and eventually stop. Will could just steadily drink and drink and drink. When we were in the pub together he used to eat crisps, one crisp at a time, with a break in between. Steady.

Anyway, as there's three of us and we all like a drink we have agreed to meet in a pub beforehand. Some clonelike chain pub as I remember. Kick-off gets closer and closer and no sign of Will. Eventually we agree we have to go. I can't remember the ticketing arrangements but it's probably pay on the gate so we don't worry. He will find us in the away end. The game kicks off, still no sign of Will. Then after about 25 minutes, we see a policeman come out of the home end "escorting" a fan. They head towards us. Sure enough, it's Will. He had arrived late so just gone in the first entrance he could find then simply asked if he could move to meet his mates. Simples!

My programme notes tell me Mark Leonard scored the only goal of the game for us and Paul Smalley was sent off for "The Iron". So we crawled through to round 4. Setting up a plum tie at home to Everton.

Seven years ago Scunthorpe and Bradford were locked in battle for promotion to the championship. It was so busy that when we played them over the Xmas period I couldn't get into my local pub (The Sparrow at the time). Whilst Bradford have fallen off disappointingly since those days, the fall has been nothing compared to the Iron. As I write they are 4th in National League North. Two tricky promotions away from the football league and playing at the likes of Rushall and Curzon (where?). But they are not alone. The league also contains Chester, Hereford,

Scarborough and Darlington. A cautionary tale to those of us who think (usually at 5pm on a Saturday) that things can't get much worse. I do hope they make it back to the league.

Manchester City

Saturday 10th December 1988. Manchester in the 80's was a dark, grim foreboding place. And that was the nice bits. Maine Road was a long walk up a dismal road away from the centre of town. It certainly felt like the epitome of Lowry football. However, the inside of the ground was immeasurably better. Festooned with the latest craze. Inflatable bananas. According to folklore Frank Newton started the trend in August 87 by taking a single 5 foot banana to a home game and dressing it in his Man City top. By December 88 things had reached epic proportions. Bury had black puddings, Stoke had pink panthers (why?) and even Grimsby had Harry the Haddock. There must have been thousands of bananas being waved at us from the stands that day. What a sight. It certainly must have distracted the Bradford players as we were awful that day. To be fair the 4-0 victory took Man City top. Everton, who weren't playing that day, as they were playing Liverpool and this had been moved to Sunday, had arranged for their players to come and watch as they were due to play us in four days time in the League Cup. They were seen laughing as they left the ground. I don't know if this was used as motivation for the Bradford team, but in a complete reversal we were awesome at Valley Parade and easily beat Everton 3-1. It's a funny old game football.

I have walked past Man City's new ground but it's not what I'm looking for – it seems lost to me in a world of corporate football. Impressive and yet soulless at the same time. And apparently a nightmare for parking and a quick escape. And I bet there isn't a decent pub. It's probably quicker for me to get home from Walsall, 80 miles away than it is to do the 15 miles back from the Etihad. That said. I will definitely go if Bradford ever get there!

I do occasionally wonder how I would feel if the oil money (or other money) turned up at my club. I don't suppose I need worry. But last week I was at a party and we were chatting about this book as I vainly try to increase sales! We turned to a guy next to us and asked if he liked football. "Oh yeah big Man City fan" He said. At least he had the decency to say Man City not just City. "I see you have just won" we replied. To which his honest response was "Have we?". Unbelievable. That's what you get when you become the dominant club I suppose. I have no choice but I am sticking with Bradford.

Oldham

At time of writing Oldham are not one of the current 92. But they have a special place in the pantheon of away grounds. It is just so cold. They say that Oldham is 6 miles outside of Manchester, and you need an extra jumper for every mile. They are not wrong. October 1989, (October, not January), finds me having agreed to meet up with Klaas behind the goal. It's a relatively normal October evening as I set off from Liverpool so I don't dress as if I am about to trek through the Arctic Circle. Big mistake. It is freezing, with ice already formed in the car park.

The honours are shared in the game and we head off (I think to a local pub?). In any case, we find ourselves back at the car park with no other cars around. The "car park" is in fact just a huge skating rink by now. Ice everywhere, October!. "Brilliant" says Klaas, we can try out our ice driving skills". To be fair, he has calmed down a lot from his youthful exuberance.

I went back to Oldham in February 2020. (February! – am I mad). I suppose I knew how to dress. But this time it was the wind that got us. The game had to be delayed by 30 minutes as an advertising hoarding had been half blown off the roof and was now dangling at a perilous angle. It sadly only took them 30 minutes to yank it down. If only our defence had shown as much resistance as the sign, it only took Oldham 30 minutes to dismantle our defence, catalysed by Anthony O'Connor's left leg collapsing to allow Oldham through clean on goal.

It would have been better if the match had been called off. Bradford were awful that day. Losing 3-0 with some truly horrendous football. Our manager Gary Bowyer took the full brunt of the packed away end. "Gary Bowyer, get out of our club" we sang. And he was gone the next day. Shame really in retrospect as we have certainly had worse managers since!

Again, there are more memories of the journey into the ground than the game itself. The 30 minute delay had been announced early and this had provided a bonus 30 minutes drinking time to the Bradford horde. Like I say we like a drink. Some of them were in a right state by the time we got to the turnstiles. One of the Bradford players appeared at the turnstiles and handed out his complimentary tickets. My son Tom needed one so he grabbed a couple. Then some guy who had clearly enjoyed the extra 30 minutes drinking asked Tom for his spare... And insisted paying for it! Tom is now £20 up on the day. Before we could explain, the guy wanders off to the turnstile and gets refused entry for being too drunk. "Go drink some coffee" say the stewards. It all ended happily though. We watched him wander off round the corner then come straight back and in through a different turnstile.

Cambridge

I don't have particularly fond memories of Cambridge, though I am sure it's a nice enough place. In May 91, Bradford were in their customary tenth place in the third tier. This does seem to be our long term average, (over my lifetime). But in early May we still had several games to catch up on and were thus in with some chance of a play-off place. Cambridge on the other hand were flying high and if the results went the right way they would get promoted this very evening and possibly even win the league. In fact, to spoil the suspense, Cambridge did go on to win the league, whilst Bradford went into the final game needing "results to go our way" and an 8-0 win. With 7th the target for play offs, we of course finished 8th. Three points off Bury so it was never going to be.

In pre sat nav days I had underestimated how far away Cambridge is from Solihull (100 miles) and we arrived late to see big queues. We headed for the turnstiles to see two long snaking queues of opposing fans. Not only were the good folk of Cambridge there in their droves to see their team promoted, the Bradford lads fancied their chances too. There seemed to be something odd about how close the away fans were queuing to the home fans. Soon some not at all good natured taunting started going on and the atmosphere was quite sour. It was notable that the closer to the turnstiles the fans got, the braver the taunts got as they prepared to duck into the safety of the home or way end. Imagine these fans surprise as we go through the turnstile and find we are all in the same end! Some genius having decided they could get more fans in the ground this way. The police valiantly ensured some sort of segregation and away we went.

In truth, Cambridge were just a bit better than us that season and despite our best attempts the game ended 2-1 to them. The expected celebration scenes for the promotion followed. However, the police had now decided that this meant trouble in the away end, especially as there wasn't really any segregation and so had decided somewhat oddly, the solution to this was to lock the doors. The only way out was to go on the pitch and out through the main stand. So we ended up in a celebration pitch invasion for an opposing team. The only pitch invasion I have ever been in. Bizarre.

The match programme is a fascinating time capsule for a bygone age. There's a full page advert for a Gary Glitter concert (ahem) and not one but two separate diatribes on the perils of a super league, including also a lovely climate change denial (not sure why that's relevant to a super league) comparing people who believe in climate change to David Icke (look him up if you don't know) and the second column ends with the strange sentence. "I got CS gassed twice in Southend once..." – Who knows what he was on about.

The programme also reminds me that in 1991/92 season the league expanded to 93 teams and there were plans to further expand to 94. This was quickly abandoned and with Aldershot going bust we were back to 92. Otherwise this book would be called 94.

Wigan (and Burnley, Preston, Peterborough and York)

Wigan was one of a large number of clubs I ticked off in the Northwest and elsewhere in the early 90's as part of a "weekend away". Drive to a ground with my girlfriend, stop in a nice pub in a nice village and have a country walk the following day. Very civilised. Football was indeed getting gentrified in the 90's.

Wigan, Mk1 at their pretty awful Springfield Park stadium, January 1992 was memorable only for having a grass bank as an option to spectate from (I hadn't seen one of those since The Shay in the 80's) and nearly getting arrested in the toilets. The toilets were as basic as usual, a long portacabin filled with one huge steel urinal. At least there was a roof. On this occasion though, I needed a sit down (as they say). I had entered through the gents door and walked all the way along the urinals, to find a single cubicle at the very far end. So in I went, and having completed my business, left via the exit immediately ahead of me. An eagle eyed policeman immediately swooped to arrest me for using the "Ladies loos". It took me a while to persuade him to stick his head inside the portacabin to see I had actually just used the loos. Separate Ladies facilities apparently not being a big thing in Wigan. And that's pretty much it for my memories of Springfield Park, and also for my memories of Preston (I think it had a plastic pitch in February 91 when I visited?), Peterborough, York and Burnley. Sorry.

I do remember my second visit to Wigan though. Wigan by now had undergone a significant upgrade, moving to the DW stadium. When you meet fans of any club they do all tend to talk with pride as if they are responsible for their clubs victories. But Wigan shows, you don't need fans to get to the premiership, just money and that is what DW had done in the intervening years. Whilst the bill for breaking into the top flight is getting higher it is still possible. You just probably need to be an oil baron now. Or maybe a Hollywood billionaire? We will see.

For a new ground it's not all that bad and the toilets are certainly better. It's a good deal too big for the appetite of the Wigan community, especially in the post premiership days. As we sang "Empty seats, empty seats, they're here, they're there, they're every f,,ing where, empty seats". My mate Tony came along, even though he was full of cold and sat looking pretty miserable for most of the game as we battled to hold a much better team 1-1. It was mid November 2017 and pretty cold. Then in the 90th minute our young and ill-fated winger Tyrrel Robinson popped up to score a screaming winner – an unlikely 2-1 win and Tony's cold was forgotten.

Fulham

I have a surprising number of friends who are Fulham fans (well two!). Unlike many football clubs, Fulham seem to have led an astonishingly charmed life. Situated on extraordinarily expensive land it has always been a prime target for property developers.

At the time of my visit in May 92 expectations were high that this could be the last ever game at Craven Cottage.

A delightful ground in a delightfully expensive location. You can see from the picture above that this is the only ground that ever let me in with my SLR camera. They know a nice camera in

Fulham. In the programme, a beaming Jimmy Hill (groan) wrote glowingly of the prospect of a ground share arrangement with Chelsea. To be fair he had already acted to stop a deeply inadvisable merger with QPR. Hill wrote that "unfortunately" the ground share couldn't start next season so there would have to be one more season at the Cottage. The club was so nervous about what the supporters might do that they had to send "celebrity fan" Radio DJ Diddy David Hamilton on to the pitch to promise that this wasn't the last ever home game, so please do not tear up the stand or the pitch at the end of the game!

Thirty years on and they are still at Craven Cottage in the hands of Shahid Khan. A man who launched a very "interesting" £600m bid to buy Wembley stadium. I would have taken the money personally. But if he had his offer accepted I wonder where Fulham would be playing now. As it is, Fulham continue, a charmed life at the Cottage. Do visit while you can.

One final thing, If like me, you want to see your own club play at all the other 91, this is always going to throw up some challenges. Teams like Bradford, Watford, Bournemouth, Northampton etc that have travelled up and down through all the leagues are the easier ones. But even so, you are likely to have some issues. For instance, as I write, only 2 clubs, Port Vale and Bradford I think have actually beaten all the other 91 in a league game. It's a tough challenge. As it happens, the toughest challenge for Bradford is Fulham. If you hadn't been to Craven Cottage by September 1993 you are still waiting.

Mansfield

"Not much matches Mansfield", or so the advert for Mansfield bitter goes (used to go?). In fact, 5 games into the season Mansfield had accumulated a totally underwhelming 2 points and were sitting second bottom, whilst Bradford had 10 points and were looking good. It's fair to say the resulting 5-2 win to Mansfield came as a shock. I haven't been back to Mansfield since, so my memories are over 30 years out of date. The place was then looking very much unloved and the years of hardship as the mines closed were still fresh to see. It will be interesting to revisit at some point.

Glancing back through the programme. There is a whole page dedicated to how to store your programme collection. It appears I've been doing it all wrong. "Chuck them in the bottom of the wardrobe for 30 years" is apparently not the approved methodology. Who knew? The article was written by the editor of "Programme monthly" magazine. I wonder if that's been featured on Have I Got News For You?

Brighton

January 1993. I was living in Birmingham and had mapped out my route to all 92 clubs. I had the poster by my desk at work. I had worked out all the drive times on "Autoroute". I had even considered where I might get jobs to get the list done more easily. An interesting way of planning a career. The map suggested to me that Brighton was going to be hard work to get to no matter where I lived in the country so I had better take my chances. I contrived a work visit to a swimming pool with a novel dehumidification system I was working on in Tunbridge Wells to coincide with a Wednesday night game at the Goldstone ground and we were off. Me and my lodger Adrian who also worked with me at British Gas. Lovely, expenses paid. Adrian was a Notts Forest fan, but for some reason prepared to put up with my desire to hit the south coast on a January evening. I have the programme in front of me now. It tells me that Brighton and Bradford in those days were absolutely identical in popularity. Around mid-table in the third tier and both averaging crowds that season of 6,700.

When you compare crowd figures from 30 years ago to today you do have to remember that crowds used to be understated – cash sales that the tax man doesn't need to see back in the 90's. Whereas todays attendances tend to be overstated as every season ticket is counted even if you actually only bother to turn up once a season and are just paying on the off chance your team hits a purple patch. Even so, Bradford and Brighton were equally non-descript in footballing terms. And as it happens Bradford would rise first. Only to fall away. And look at Brighton now. Oh to have an owner with the clubs interests at heart, a well-run club and a succession of good managers. I can only look on with envy.

The game itself was a totally unmemorable 1-1 draw. Before the game we had taken to the beach as all away fans surely do? Adrian had then realised that a thin jumper was probably not enough for a January evening, even on the south coast, and bought an emergency top in the local market. Most memorable really was the journey home. A good 160 mile drive at 10 O'clock at night – should at least be quiet on the roads right? How annoying is it to be sat in a contra flow on the M25 at midnight with 100 miles still to go. Sad to say that this has now become a regular event on mid-week games. Why are we so slow at road repairs in this country?

Pat reminds me we went back to see a 0-0 draw here with Chris (Brighton fan) in attendance. The only game where we had an ice cream before the game. Again it was a pretty dull game but the ball kept going out over the ridiculously small stand along one touchline into a neighbouring garden From the away end we could see an old man watching from his garden behind this stand - cries of "One Victor Meldrew, there's only one Victor Meldrew". Things have really moved on for Brighton.

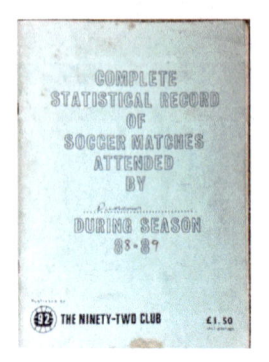

Brighton, Good luck to them. I haven't been back and the new ground looks like everything I hate – maybe I will find out one day.

Stoke

I have a huge pile of programmes from my early years, before the internet meant you didn't crave football content so much. Flicking back through them it turns out that I seem to have seen Stoke play a very large number of times. I don't know why this is. But it's interesting to see that Peter Fox apparently was always in goal for them. Fox in fact played for Stoke from 1978 to 1993. But I wonder if there is even more we are not seeing? Some kind of Dorian Gray story may be there if we look deeper? The Bradford Stoke programme from 1991, when of course Fox was in goal, takes a look back at previous meetings. Sure enough, the first ever meeting between Bradford and Stoke was in 1907 and guess the name of the Stoke keeper that day, yes you got it, Fox. This could be a case for Mulder and Scully?

I've always found Stoke a strange place. It's not really got a city centre, it's an accumulation of 7 towns (Just like Rome, my Stoke friends tell me.) My first visit was 14th January 1989. It was to be my first sighting of two players who would become Bradford legends in very different ways. Chris Kamara and Peter Beagrie. Beagrie was one of the two players we had "wanted" after our own winger/striker John Hendrie left. The other being David Currie. As it turned out we just had the ten years to wait to get Beagrie.

The thing that struck me on the day was how heavily policed everything was. I had driven down from Liverpool with my expensive SLR camera in the hope of taking some pictures. "Not a chance" chorused the police and stewards as one. Apparently, I might be bringing a £200 camera to throw at someone? Back to the car boot goes the camera.

I have checked my notes (in 1988 I have bought myself, a little optimistically, a 92 club booklet to record all my games). By January I have been to 33 games in the season. Quite an effort for a student. I don't remember anything about the game now other than the inflatable pink panthers. But you will be pleased to know Peter Fox was in goal for Stoke. The heavy policing continued after the game as I was trying to drive to the M6. You can't go that way said the transport police. "But I'm trying to get to Liverpool". This seemed to completely flummox them and they waved me through.

So much for the Victoria Ground, now sadly gone. I have since had the misfortune to visit the new abomination. Here's a genius idea, let's build a stadium with no parking, situated on a dual carriageway, on the ring road and the main route north of Birmingham and south of Manchester from the M6 to the M1. No pubs, nowhere near town or a train station and nowhere to park. I'd love to see the travel plan. I have a very good friend who is a Stoke fan "Oh yeah, it's a nightmare" is all he can add.

Newcastle

Newcastle, like Norwich, is a lovely city, miles and miles (by English standards) from anywhere else. I do like Newcastle a lot. An abundance of good pubs, an easy walk to the ground and friendly locals. Unfortunately I haven't yet seen Bradford there. My one visit was in April 89 to see a relegation bound Newcastle play Liverpool. John Hendrie was playing for Newcastle so that gave me something to cheer from the Gallowgate end. But the undoubted star of the show that day was their Brazilian striker Mirandinha. We stood on the open terracing with the Geordies and roared as Mirandinha slotted a worldie home. The game eventually ending 2-2.

This was a month or so after Xmas and I had pestered my mum into buying me a hand held mobile TV. 1989! Who needs a smartphone. I had gone with my mate Jem, a Geordie and we were walking back to town to look for some good beer. I was keen to find out how Bradford had got on. In truth the TV was useless to watch but it did act as a decent enough radio and it had a massive aerial so everyone knew (or thought) I was listening to the radio and thus likely to know the scores. Some Geordie came up to me and said something entirely unintelligible in his broad accent. I looked blank. "How did Sunderland get on?" Jem translated. Crisis averted. I'm afraid I can't remember how Sunderland got on, but I'm guessing assuming this random stranger is still alive he's pretty happy with how it's going for Newcastle and Sunderland at the moment.

Like I say, lovely ground, lovely pubs, nice people. I really hope to be back. Which takes us to another North East team.

Middlesbrough

Travelling by supporters coach gives quite a blinkered perspective to an away ground. In theory you can't drink on the coach (ahem). The bus may stop right outside the ground and coming home you are straight back in. At Tranmere the coach is so close to the exit that you can barely get past it if you want to go find your car. I know at Crawley, the Bradford bus stops in the town centre near the nice pubs these days but I've never seen that anywhere else. There's often a good atmosphere and sometimes a dodgy atmosphere on board. I have seen (for instance) a full on porn movie on one coach, 1 girl travelling ("you don't mind do you love" – a statement really not a question from the instigator) and one young lad ("Don't tell your mum") said the guy in charge... I far prefer making my own way. There are some times though when you do consider the coach as a good option. Middlesborough had a reputation for being an unpleasant place to visit, we certainly weren't going to be sight-seeing. But in the end we chose to drive. This turned out to be a good decision. Boro were pushing for promotion whilst we were fighting in vain against relegation. We lost 2-0. Klaas and I scurried back to the car through the dismal streets around Ayresome park (maybe it's nice now?) and hot tailed it back home. Good move. It turned out the supporters club coaches got bricked on the way home. Why?

I haven't been to the new ground yet. I hope it's better?

Hartlepool

Staying in the North East for one more club. You can't write about Hartlepool without mentioning the monkey. The club and the town have embraced the apocryphal story of the "monkey hanging" to heart so much that their mascot is a monkey in a Pools shirt called H'Angus. In 2002 a candidate going under the name of H'Angus was elected mayor of the town! If you don't have a clue what I'm on about. The story goes that during the Napoleonic period a French ship was wrecked in a storm off the coast. The only survivor was the ship's pet monkey. Mistaking this for a Frenchman (simpler times) the locals immediately hung the monkey. And it's been "monkey hangers" ever since,

We visited Hartlepool on boxing day 1991. A 3pm kick off but still requiring floodlights. Sure enough as the game progressed one of the lights failed. A man was dispatched to try and fix them to a delighted chorus of "Theres a monkey on the lights". I think both sets of fans joined in.

The Bradford team sheet makes interesting reading for that game. In total we had 5 strikers in the starting line up. Mark Leonard, Frank Stapleton, Sean McCarthy, Steven Torpey and Paul Jewell. In fact, Leonard was playing in defence and Stapleton and Jewell in midfield. It was a very make do and mend squad that season as our decline continued. We were 17th going into that game. We lost 1-0. Hartlepool are currently in the national league but they have a good set of fans. I hope they make it back soon.

Exeter, Port Vale and Orient

In the interregnum between the Klaas years and the Pat years I had decided to further my career with a job move. I had received my job offer and duly handed my 1 month notice in to leave Solihull behind. Needless to say there was plenty of time on my hands so what better way to use it than to tick off a few grounds. Now, where are Bradford playing:

Exeter first, Saturday 3rd April. Great, weekend away, a good look round a pretty city and a walk on Dartmoor. On the day it was absolutely chucking it down and the away end was an open terrace. The delightful stewards opened the gates for us and let us sit in the covered seats. Lovely guys. It seemed almost rude when we won 1-0. But we weren't complaining and this unexpected 3 points boosted us to an unlikely outside shot at the play offs. Next up Port Vale. Tuesday 13th April. Old fashioned away game. Call Klaas, meet behind goal. Home by last orders. Win 2-1. Blimey, these play offs are in view.

Final new place for me, just before the new job. Leyton Orient, 1st May. Orient is a hell of a drag to get to from most places. But by now you can almost sniff those elusive play-offs. We couldn't, could we? We are 7th, one place off the play offs, but annoyingly Orient are 8th, right behind us. It's rare for me to pick out one player in an opposing team, but that day, Ricky Otto was just too good for us. It was a hell of a game but we lost 4-2 and that was the play off dream done for another season. Barry Fry, no less rated Otto enough to sign him for a £100k a week or so later. But his career never really blossomed from there. He was great that day though.

I haven't been back to Exeter or Orient, but I have been back to Port Vale. I would say that if you are going. Go early. Not only are there some great pubs, it's also worth sampling some of their excellent Oatcakes from one of the local shops. Don't miss out.

THE PAT YEARS

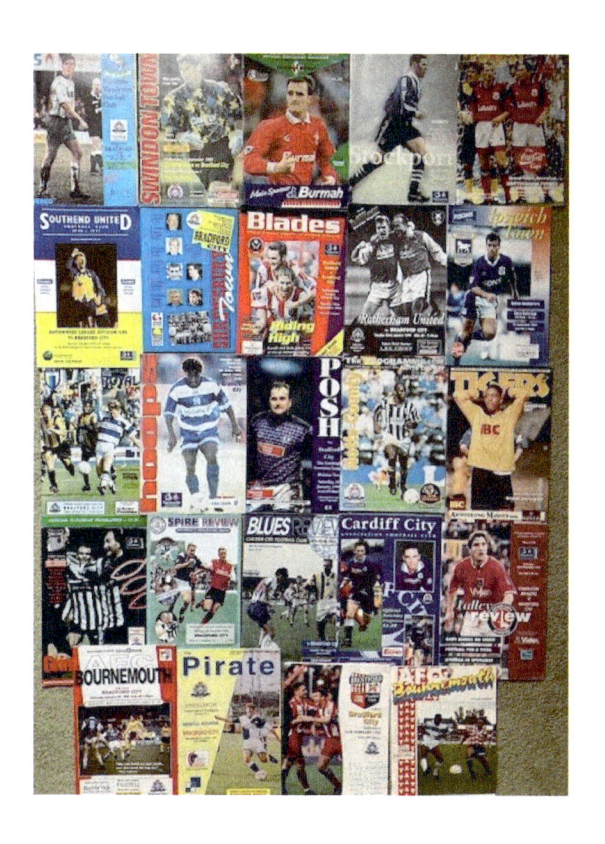

Section 2 - The Pat Years 1994 – 2005

In 1993, British Gas were looking to relocate me to Loughborough. They sent us on familiarisation trips to entice us to move there. This probably worked well for the older employees who could afford the lovely villages around the countryside, but all I could afford was the Town Centre and I really didn't like what I saw. So much so that I changed jobs and ended up working in Swindon (Frying pan and fire?). Anyway, a new area of the country to base my football travels from. And I really couldn't believe my luck when Pat turned up in the graduate intake programme for 1994. A Bradfordian with a shared passion for the team. Let's get that motor started!

Swansea

I visited the Vetch twice in quick succession in the early 90's and the memories have to some extent blurred with time so I will treat them as one experience with two journeys. The first trip was 26th September 1992. I was living in Birmingham and starved of friends to watch football with. So I resorted to convincing my girlfriend of the time to combine a weekend away with a football trip. In this case a lovely trip to the Brecon beacons and a minor detour to catch the game. The second trip was 7th October 1995 and by then I was living in Swindon and had Pat to take to the game. I think we also took Mark (yet another one, this time a York fan).

The pubs are worth a mention – we found a lovely pub (name now lost in the mists of time) and unusually decided we liked it so much we returned for another drink after the game, quite unusual even at the time and these days my bladder would definitely not be up for that kind of thing with a long drive home. It's not as far home as Bradford but still well over a 100 miles.

We were casually drinking after the game, three lads sat together in our mid 20's, clearly having been to the game, when a young lad of similar age came for a chat. After a few pleasantries he had established we were Bradford fans and kindly enquired if we knew any fans who were up for a fight – this could all be arranged for the next meeting if we fancied it. All very pleasant and quite sinister at the same time. My mate Pat – a mild mannered teacher does seem to be a bit of a magnet for this sort of thing, but I guess no harm done. On the way out we bumped into another group of lads on a "session" and one of them was John Hartson, who would have been playing for Arsenal at the time if not injured. The fitness regime seems to have moved on since the 90's, unless your Jack Grealish.

The Vetch itself was an interesting stadium, with one half of the ground looking like a contender for National Stadium whilst our end looked poor by non league standards. The toilets also didn't fail to disappoint – you had to wade through ankle deep "liquid" to get to the urinals. There was water dripping from a cave like ceiling. Lovely. This being the early 90's away following this far away from home was sparse. There will have been some fans sat down, but on the terraces I counted 11 fans and three of these were Leeds fans on a stag do. One of the 11 was a rather corpulent individual and there really is no place to hide when attendance is that sparse. The home fans took to singing "you wanna go on a diet" all in their beautifully trained Welsh singing voices. Quite delightful.

Pat tells me this was the game when he finally realised he was not going to make it as a professional footballer as Des Hamilton was significantly younger (and better) than him. I think it is safe to say that this realisation about my own talent came to me a very large number of years earlier. But I do hold the record for having scored from the corner flag of all four corners of the 5-a-side pitch in the Swindon Oasis Centre.

Halifax and Hereford

Two teams who have suffered greatly over the intervening years, but who are both, hopefully on their way back now. Halifax are currently in a play off spot in the national league so it could be next season. Hereford are a bit lower, mid table in National league north. But good luck to them both. Both excellent away venues. Hereford has a range of nice pubs worth a visit and they had the "Mappa Mundi" on display at the cathedral when I visited. So culture too!

Halifax, I have been to many times. Another town with a great range of pubs. They were one of the "Friday night teams". It used to be popular for smaller teams with larger local rivals to play on a Friday night. Thus allowing the fans to see both the smaller team and the bigger team. Tranmere used to do this all the time.

The pop music poster boys for Tranmere are the band Half Man Half Biscuit and they famously refused an appearance on the pop TV programme the Tube because they would have missed a home game. I am told they were offered a helicopter back (it was filmed in Newcastle I think?) but they would have missed the first half so it was no deal! I would love to hear Tranmere run out to a Half Man Half Biscuit song. National Shite day perhaps? "There's a man with a mullet going mad with a mallet in Millets" – Genius Lyrics.

Anyway, back to Halifax. For me it meant that I could drive home for the weekend, stop off in Halifax on a Friday night and see their game and then watch Bradford on the Saturday. I did this around 5 or 6 times over two seasons in the late 80's. I think Sky has done for this tradition now games kick off at all sorts of times. I used to quite enjoy a Friday night game.

Oxford United

I first visited Oxford in February 1992. I had a friend at University there so it seemed a good chance to tick off a ground. Second tier bottom club Oxford were entertaining second bottom Newcastle. A real 6 pointer! The game lives on in my memory for one reason only, the fog. The game was pretty much watchable (probably) if you were sat by the halfway line but we were behind the goal. The game ended with a high scoring 5-2 win for Oxford. But time and again the only way we knew a goal had been scored was when the ref popped back in sight at the half way line and restarted the game with a kick-off. I think in total we saw 2 of the 7 goals.

Two years later and I was living just down the road in Swindon. Pat and I were back at the Manor Ground with depressing regularity. Parking in Stapleton road in honour of our manager and driving past the famous "shark in the roof" in Headington. March 95 lost 1-0. March 96 lost 2-0. September 96 lost 2-0. September 97 and things are on the up for Bradford with the Richmond money – drew 0-0. Hurrah! Then finally, of course after I have moved away from Swindon, so I am not there to see it. In December 98 we finally managed a goal, and a win! 1-0. Typical. Pat tells me he was at that game. Good for him!

Apart from the absolute goal festival I only really have two memories of Oxford.

For some reason we were hanging out by the away entrance at one of the games when one of our players appeared and said

"Some spare tickets for the game lads – enjoy". It was Graham Mitchell, one of our adequate players at the time, who in truth hadn't been playing all that well recently. But everyone loves a free ticket "Brilliant – Thanks Mitch – you playing today?" – "No" and off he trudges.

The other memory – which other Bradford fans of a 90's vintage might also remember was of Pat's brother's girlfriend, Ivona, a merchant banker. All of this quite sophisticated for us. She had come to the game in an unfeasibly tight pair of blindingly white pants. The Bradford fans hadn't seen the like and it was great fun to hover backwards and listen in to the conversations. Much more fun than the game – that's for sure!

Swindon

As I mentioned, 1993 saw me relocate for work and end up in Swindon, just as the team were looking forward to their first ever premier league season. It didn't last. I did pop along once to see them play Spurs but they were outclassed and by January when I visited, already 7 points adrift of safety. By the 95/96 season they were back in the third tier with Bradford, but like Oxford, Swindon was not a happy hunting ground for us. September 95 we lost 4-1. January 97 we drew 1-1, And for my last game November 97 we lost 1-0. Again, as with Oxford, as soon as I moved away and didn't attend, our form transformed. Winning 4-1 at Swindon in December 98. Maybe I should just accept I jinx some things?

I do have one happy memory of the County Ground. Pat's brother Eddie had gained a reputation for turning up right on the stroke of kick off. We would joke that the ref would wait for a signal from him before the game could commence. Sure enough, it happened that the kick off was delayed until 3-15 for delays on the motorway (Eddie came by train). And, of course Eddie turned up at exactly 3.15. "Right Ref, we can kick off now!".

Pat and I took our bosses to one of the games. Polite young things that we were in the workplace, they saw a different side of us that evening. I haven't taken a boss to a game since. You can reveal too much of your character sometimes.

Bristol Rovers (And City)

A nice local trip for me. Bristol Rovers were housed at Twerton park for my entire Swindon stay, just down the road in Bath. It was to turn out this was yet another unlucky ground for us. In my first visit we took the lead three times and lost 4-3. In fact, that was as good as it got. After that, Lost 4-3, Lost 4-0, Lost 1-0. I have since been back to the clubs "new ground" now at least in Bristol. We lost 2-1.

The 4-0 loss was one of my first away days with Pat. I got a great insight into his character that day. I think we were 2-0 down at the time. The Rovers guy rounds the keeper and is through clean on goal. "Miss" shouts Pat. "There's always hope". There wasn't!

Twerton was a distinctly "non league" operation. It did give a beautiful view of the town. It also gave a magnificent view of the very large gas tank in the middle of Bath that some planning genius had approved. Incredibly, when all the "gasometers" were removed the Bath mayor at the time tried to start a campaign to keep the tank. As the Bath Preservation Trust commented somewhat sardonically "the gasometer is not one of the reasons Bath is a World Heritage Site"! The views of this possibly splendid sight did prompt the Bristol City fans to nickname the Rovers fans "gas heads". To which the Rovers fans quickly responded by nicknaming City fans "Shit heads". That's proper football banter.

I only visited Bristol City once. It was a large ground fallen on hard times , or so it felt. The locals seemed to struggle to believe they were reduced to these levels. As a Bradford fan I know how they felt. We lost 2-1 that day. All I remember is Mark Stallard had a particularly poor game that day so I gave him some abuse. He'd only scored 1 goal in the 6 games since we signed him and he looked out of touch to me. Maybe it worked? He scored in each of his next 4 outings. Bagging another 3 in the later stages of the season and scoring in the play off final to promote us. I told you I am no scout!

As usual, I do remember the pub. I had one of my ambitious beer guide days and dragged Pat to the Smythe arms. It was miles from the ground! Sorry Pat.

West Brom

Here is a ground I would become very familiar with in the 90's but in fact it all started in September 89. My time in Liverpool was drawing to a close. My PhD was due to be finished soon and I would have to get a job. Of course I didn't know at this point that I would end up just down the road in Solihull. So I jumped at the chance for a solo trip down the M6 on a Tuesday night to tick off a new ground. League Cups were often two leg affairs back then and this was the first leg. Bradford weren't in any great form at the time but produced a compelling performance on the night to win 3-1. "Jobs a good un", so I thought, and even better, a little exuberant youthful driving saw me back in Liverpool in time for last orders. Bradford managed to lose the second leg 5-3 to go out on away goals and that was probably the high point of the season done, Unbelievable Jeff.

More unbelievable luck was to follow. I was quickly back at the Hawthorns in March 90 to preside over the final diggings of a relegation campaign as we lost 2-0. The only use this game had in my mind was that I knew the ground layout, thoroughly, where to park etc. I also knew the away end had a very big roof. Oh yes a lovely big roof.

FEBRUARY 92. I emphasise February. I am living in Birmingham (well Solihull) and Bradford are due at the Hawthorns. "I don't fancy it, it will be cold" said my girlfriend – not entirely unreasonably. "It will be fine, they have a roof on the away end. I've been before" I reassure. So off we go, queuing in the heavy sleet to pay our £3's and longing for the shelter of that lovely big roof. What a treat to find.... The roof has been dismantled in the name of "ground improvements". Oldham aside I have never been so cold in my entire life. The car heater on full blast did not touch it and I had to soak in a hot bath for a very long time before I could regain some sense of humanity. Apparently, the game ended 1-1. I have no idea! I don't think my girlfriend ever came to another game after that.

But there's more. March 93 finds me sat in the home end and I have unwisely agreed to view this years offering with a good friend who happens to be a baggies fan. The game ends 2-2 which tests both our resolves to look calm and relatively composed. This is my first experience of Bradford from the wrong end, so possibly good training?

But there's more. October 96 sees us well into the Pat years. By now Pat has moved back to Oxford University to do teacher training and I am used to driving to his place to pick him up for away games. The bright lights of West Brom beckon. I arrive at Pat's place to meet Helen "Just a friend". Oh yes Pat – "Just a friend" – "She is wearing your Bradford shirt"!. Needless to say, Pat and Helen have been happily married now for over 20 years. "Just a friend". Being a first date we took her to the delightful pubs of Handsworth and then to a local kebab shop for the specialty "Meat and Chips". Don't ask what sort of "meat"! And all for only 50p.

Pat has his own memories of this ground. He went on his own before he had met me. Visiting the urinals at the tender age of about 20 he was horrified to discover he was passing pure blood. I'm guessing the other guys in the urinals were a bit taken aback too. He was quickly diagnosed with bladder cancer (about the youngest in the country) and a credit to our health service was completely cured. I think he was the first person ever to be signed off by Oxford hospital as cured of bladder cancer. That certainly puts the football in perspective.

Bournemouth

Life can be a bit of a lottery. In some ways I wouldn't be surprised if I'd never been to Bournemouth and was still waiting to tick it off my list. In fact, I've been three times. All in the 90's. My initial , pre-football, 1980's impressions of Bournemouth were not favourable. I went there on a motorbike holiday in 1986. We stopped in the local Tourist Information Centre to enquire where we could stay "No where round here – no one wants bikers" – lovely. We ended up camping in the New Forest which I'm sure was much nicer.

My first trip to Dean Court was in September 1990. We drove down from Birmingham through local villages (no motorways here) and I got a speeding fine as I failed to slow in time for one of the small villages en-route. We lost 3-1. What a great day. My second trip was in August 1993. I had just started living in Swindon, so Bournemouth wasn't far away right?, Wrong, with no motorways it was quite some trek. But we drew 1-1 so at least that was a step in the right direction. My third and final trip was in January 1996. I am now, unbelievably, working with 2 Bournemouth fans, so there's quite a group of us going down to this one. There really is nowt to choose between the teams, so of course we lose 3-1 again.

Bournemouth's average attendance in the second tier last season was 9,500. Bradford's in the fourth tier is almost double that. I can only look on in envy at what can be achieved at a well run club. And bemoan the fact that we haven't had a well run club for 7 years.

Plymouth and Chester

Eh? Not the most obvious pairing of football grounds perhaps. But when the 94/95 season fixtures came out, it was to be Chester and then Plymouth for me. First up was Chester away, combine that with a quick trip up north to my mums and say happy birthday, perfect. I always went back home around her birthday as it used to always be near the start of the season. 13th August that year. These days the season starts earlier than that so most people now can't get their summer holidays in before the season starts. Next up would be Plymouth away on 27th August. Not that close to Swindon (160 miles) but it seems closer!

On the way to the ground we saw our chairman Geoffrey Richmond in his dark green Bentley. He always gave a rather regal wave when he saw the claret and amber scarves going past. Generally a good omen. His car was instantly recognisable with the number plate "1 GR". The plate was sold off at auction in 2003. I wonder who owns it now?

Let's be honest, we all go into the first game with a lovely mix of trepidation and excitement. Who are the new players? Will they gel? Is this the year? Well, it couldn't have started better that year. A Paul Jewell (later to become our manager and guide us to the premier league) hat trick plus a goal from super Johnny Taylor helped us to a handsome 4-1 away win at Chester. I think this was the biggest away win I had seen to date. Theres a quirk at Chester that part of the ground is actually in Wales. This meant that during COVID, when English football reopened but Welsh football didn't. They were actually breaking the law by playing a game. I don't think they got prosecuted?

We had won one game, we were over excited, dreams of running away with the title, over 100 points, all the usual early season stupidity. In the next 3 games, without my help (?) Bradford beat Grimsby home and away in the League Cup and beat Orient in the league. What a start.

My mate Chris (Brighton fan) tagged along for the day trip to Plymouth. Chris is one of those football fans who hates to see his mates teams do well. I respect him for this, it has a brutal honesty. He came along, confident that Bradford were due to trip up and he would have 160 miles to crow about it on the way home. He couldn't have been more wrong. Bradford went one better, another Jewell hat trick and a brace for Carl Shutt seeing us romp home 5-1. Chris was spitting feathers.

And I'm afraid that's pretty much where the fairy tale season ended. Jewell had 8 goals in 5 games. I think he only got half a dozen more all season. We lost our very next game 2-0 at home to Oxford and quickly sunk back to our natural mid table position. By the end of March our new owner Big Friendly Geoffrey, or was it Big Fat Geoffrey? (BFG) cleared out all the deadwood and we cruised home on a paper thin squad to the end of the season. BFG was girding his financial loins for a promotion push all the way to the premier league. We would have laughed at you if you'd told us it would work.

My memory may be playing me tricks again here? But my memory is always of BFG overtaking us in his Big Fat Bentley on the way to the ground, not us overtaking him. I have probably already implied that I would be going at a decidedly decent speed, so BFG was certainly a man going places in a hurry.

Notts Forest

When The Saint & Greavsie hit the screens in 1985, we all loved it. You could laugh at football – who knew. The grand tradition was carried into the 90's by Baddiel and Skinner. We should really get something similar going now. Football needs to be laughed at. Maybe Micah Richards could team up with someone? Anyway, as it turns out, Greavsie was commentating on this game and it really wasn't his best night as I found out watching the extended highlights (many times!) later on. This was the Coca Cola Cup second round second leg. Third tier Bradford had stunned fancy dan premier league Forest with a tremendous performance in the first leg and were 3-1 up going into stoppage time. A late goal for Forest ended the game 3-2 so they were still favourites but they had had fair warning.

Stuart Pearce was famed for his no nonsense aggressive style. I wonder how he would get on in todays football? On the night Stuart went for a crunching tackle with our right back and the pair absolutely destroyed the advertising hoardings. Both stand up, shake hands and get on with it. Stuart Pearce captained the forest team with a whole range of premiership stars of the day, Steve Stone, Neil Webb, Jason Lee (Don't mention pineapples) and it showed. Forest totally outplayed Bradford in the first half and went into half time 1-0 up, level on aggregate. The second half started differently and for 15 minutes Bradford turned on the style, eventually equalizing. This stung Forest into life and they again dominated, slotting a second in to level the tie on aggregate once more. With the tie evenly balanced and heading towards injury time lets go over to Greavsie on the box. Greavsie the ex prolific striker, had taken a dislike to Ian Ormondroyd and had spent the entire game criticising him. In these days where a lot of players are well over 6 foot it seems incredible that this 6 foot 4 inch striker "stood out" so much for being tall. But sticks was certainly getting grief from Greavsie. Maybe it was inevitable then. A super cross into the box in the 88th minute finds Ian about 12 yards out and still with work to do. He gets above the ball brilliantly and heads the ball down on to the ground to bounce over Mark Crossley's despairing dive, scenes in the away end for the 4,000 travelling fans including me and Pat.

Whilst on the telly, all Greavsie can manage on commentary is "Oh dear!".

Bradford hold out for the small amount of time left and its wild celebrations in the away end. We eventually leave the ground happily singing "You can shove the premier league up yer arse". Incredible to think that in less than 4 years we would be playing in the premier league.

Unusually for us, we decided to head to the pub for a post match celebration. This was especially unusual as we had a three hour drive ahead of us to get back to Swindon and this was a Wednesday – so a "school night". We went to the wonderful Larwood & Voce, situated, not unsurprisingly by the cricket ground. Walking back to the car two forest fans saw us and for no apparent reason, offered us a fight. It's always Pat!. We politely declined and headed off home. In bed by 3 am.

Cardiff

A word at this moment about football hooliganism. I must have been to over a thousand games now and the amount of trouble I have seen is minimal. Bradford v Leeds at Odsal. Hull v Bradford as you will read later. And that's about it. Most teams supporters are welcoming and whilst I don't always travel in club colours to away games I feel safe most of the time when I do. There are a small number of clubs where this is not the case. Millwall of course, but also, back in the 90s at their old ground, Cardiff was a very unpleasant place to visit. Living in Swindon it's an easy drive along the M4 to Cardiff on a Tuesday night to see my team in March 1995 and having been used to the genteel delights of Wycombe, Swindon and Oxford perhaps I was a little unprepared.

At the time Bradford were going nowhere, occupying our customary long term average position of tenth in the third tier. Cardiff were in a bit of relegation bother and had a poor team. In a surprisingly free flowing game Bradford take a 3-2 lead heading towards the end of the match and with a couple of minutes left our spectacularly average striker Neil Tolson[2] (63 games 12 goals) receives the ball at the edge of the box and unleashes what can only be described as a "worldie". Happy scenes in the away end and I'm looking forward to an easy drive home and bed by 11. Work in the morning. Not a bit of it. The exit doors are firmly locked. Following the Bradford fire this always causes a fair amount of consternation for our fans, But the police (not the stewards!) are adamant. "You don't want to go out there boyos" – They may not have actually said boyos, but that's what I remember. And it was close to 11 by the time we were finally allowed out to head off home.

I have been back to Cardiff city centre many times and it's a lovely city. But I haven't been back for the football. The new ground looks pretty good actually. I wonder if the fans have changed? I know Bradfords fans have, so maybe it is just how things used to be.

Brentford, Wycombe and Notts County

Back in the 90's there were two indispensable tools for the committed away fan who didn't want to end up in a petrol station asking for directions. The Good Beer Guide, which I still use today and the Football Fans Guide. Now replaced by online

---

[2] I think I sound a little harsh here on "Tolley". Lets be honest, I would love to experience the rush he must have felt when he scored that goal and all the other goals. Oh, to have been good enough and fit enough. It must be a tremendous feeling.

tools. My Fans guide from 95 can be seen below – looking remarkably dog eared and containing my notes on away pubs such as Rotherham "Moulders Rest" – Ok, Wolves – Try Yates Wine Bar, Peterborough "The Bridge" tick.

You used to be able to "spot" a lot more away fans on the motorways back in the 90's than you do today. My mate has a theory that this is because modern electric windows make it harder to dangle your scarf out of the side of the car. He may be right. I also think people do travel a bit more incognito, with less dangling paraphernalia in the back window. Though if you stop at a motorway services the fans will all be there and very noticeable. Last season it felt like we stumbled across the entirety of the Stockport away fans at the M6 Toll services. All very friendly though.

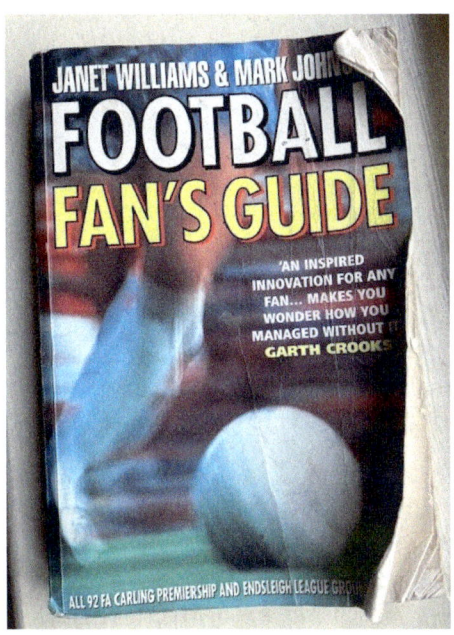

In my first two seasons with Pat I was in a whirl of ticking off new grounds, not every ground springs to mind with equal clarity and these three grounds didn't register much. Here's what I remember.

Brentford. It did indeed have a pub on every corner. We had a quick walk around the ground to confirm this fact to ourselves. But they were all packed so we went elsewhere.

While we are on Brentford, let's talk about Ivan Toney. The first time I saw him play was for Peterborough against Bradford. It only took me 5 minutes to fall in love. We should sign this guy I said, but he was way out of our league, literally.

He is now serving an 8 month ban for 232 breaches of betting rules. 232!. At least he did it properly. We are so hypocritical in football when it comes to betting. We allow clubs to plaster betting advertisements everywhere and then get all sanctimonious if a footballer actually has a bet. I don't get betting. I put a bet on once on a football match (Everton v Watford FA Cup final 1984) and it ruined the game for me. But it is clearly an addiction for some. Watch the excellent documentary Paul Merson did on his gambling addiction for a better insight than I can give. For me, we need to remove gambling adverts from the game. If that makes the top clubs a little poorer, so much the better. Maybe it will come? I have just rewatched James Hunt winning the formula 1 in 1976 and it seems strangely antiquated that all the sponsors were cigarette companies. Who knows.

Wycombe. This game was just down the road from Swindon. So Pat and I went three times (or actually 4, but only three times to successfully see a game). It's a nice place when I have visited for non football activities but the ground is one of these "awful end of the industrial estate" places so little to record other than it was another place Pat and I drove to, only to find the game was off. It's so great having mobile phones these days!

Notts County I remember was an impressive ground, but it was just empty. There were 6,100 there that day in 1995. I have just been back (2023) and this time there were just under 12,000. The thing that stood out on my second visit was how quiet the home fans were. They raced to a 4-0 lead by half time and barely made a noise, come on, what are you like when you are losing. They managed to tick most of my boxes for a bad away day. The

Wetherspoons wasn't letting away fans in (really?), they had no pies in the ground, (How can this be? You know how many tickets you have sold) and we got a side of the ground rather than an end. I don't really understand why a home team wants both ends? As a home fan, how do you decide which end to stand in? We had an end in 1995!

The one good thing was there was plenty of free parking 5 minutes away in the lovely park by the river.

When you travel to distant away games you will see a small band of regular fans. You never speak to them (it seems) but you know them by sight. Back in the 90's the regulars, decanting from the supporters coach would include two teenage girls, a small group of middle aged men and "carrier bag man". In the 90's it was always a Morrisons bag. Tragically, carrier bag man died travelling to Barnsley for an away game. RIP Kenny. I haven't seen any of the other regulars for a long time. Maybe I just don't recognise them?

These days, away day regulars include Lenny (ex City Gent mascot, and now of course a lot slimmer), Darren, who I seem to remember City Gent fanzine describe as the world's daftest man once?. I last saw Darren looking for a bus stop outside MK Dons stadium. Bucket hat man (like I say I never seem to talk to any of these people!). And of course, Charlie. Every club presumably has a Charlie? He wears his passions with pride. He can often be seen being "interviewed" by away stewards as his passions ignite. I love him for this. Now in his 70's he does not appear to be calming down. Good for you Charlie. Keep shouting.

Why don't we chat to each other more? I suppose a lot of fans are in their own "bubble" and don't welcome any intrusion. On away games I am much more likely to strike up a conversation with the home fans than the Bradford fans. From Colchester to Tranmere the home fans are interested in how your club are doing and what is happening. Maybe there is a shared player to ask about. It's good banter and of course, before the game there is little to be unhappy about! But even after the game I have had decent chats with the away fans, seasoned with a bit of ribbing about the events of the day. But still good fun. Once after a Bradford game at Oxford Pat and I headed to a pub and there were two young Bradford lads playing pool. We tried to start up a conversation and they made it pretty clear they'd be happy to thump us if we didn't go away. Always Pat. Just don't try and break the bubble, I guess.

Crewe

Stockport County used to sing a song that ended "And we're not that fond of Crewe". Tame stuff for a football song about your only Cheshire rivals. I think Crewe used to be everyone's favourite "plucky little team". Always capable of punching slightly above their weight and bringing some high quality players through the ranks. Since the Barry Bennell incidents came to light and Dario Gradi was stripped of his MBE this may have been tarnished somewhat . Like Crewe's slightly tarnished reputation I also have both some good and some not so good memories.

Its February 1995. After 5 or 6 lean years Bradford are showing a few signs of recovery. To be precise, it's a Tuesday night, I'm full of cold, but Pat is desperate to go. Come on Dunc I'll drive. It's a 135 mile drive and you have to get past the M5/M6 junction but Pat is not to be deterred. He is desperate to see our new player Etienne Verveer. "I have been pleased with the technical quality of the players" he recently crowed on his arrival "But clearly I am the most skilled". Well, how could you resist. I wrap myself in my warmest winter gear and prepare to sleep through the evenings drive. Bradford take a 1-0 lead thanks to John Taylor essentially kicking the ball out of the keepers hands and with time running out we are looking to run the clock down. Etienne has not done much so far to justify my cold ridden trip in February. Then he gets the ball about 35 yards out. Dribbles a mazey run to the corner flag. Does a couple of keepie ups. Beats the defenders, dribbles all the way around the penalty area to the other corner flag and does the same again before being dumped unceremoniously on his arse by the less than ecstatic Crewe defence. Awesome. Well worth the trip.

Of course, it's never all good times. My last visit was one of those times where nothing works out. It was near the end of the 22/23 season and a win could see us promoted automatically. I've spotted a really promising pub a mile from the ground. I'm driving Tony, my sons Sam and Eddie and also my wife as she likes a beer. I have promised a nice beer and then she is going to get the train home while we watch the game. My other son is meeting us by train in plenty of time for a pint. As we head to the ground the phone pings. My son's train is cancelled. He's not getting to the ground until near kick off time. So that ruins our logistics. Right, park near the pub, have some drinks and then drive back near the ground. We enter the pub, 10 real ales on hand pull as promised. Between us we must have tried 8 of them in two rounds. They were all horrible. Like they hadn't washed the pipes properly. Great. Now into the car and try to park near the station and ground, to meet Tom. Of course, its chaos as there are a load of Bradford fans in town and also a surprisingly large number of Crewe fans seeing as they have nothing to play for. We scramble somewhere to park and wonder where Tom is. Unknown to me, in the scramble to get everyone sorted my DAB radio gets knocked out of the car and lost – I'm £60 down at this point. But it gets worse. We head into the ground. Tom wants a drink as he hasn't had one. Sam is always up for another drink. "Sorry, we don't serve alcohol when the away end is full" – What? I mean, what ! Thats tremendous economic thinking.

But it can still get worse. As mentioned, a win could see Bradford fight into the automatic promotion spots. But Crewe are up for the challenge and the Bradford players seem a bit scared. On top of this, some of our idiot fans have decided to have a go at our ex-player Kelvin Mellor. I don't know why, he did his best for us in a poor team in an awful season. But have you ever seen this work? Nine times out of 10 it just motivates the player to do better. Sure enough Crewe race to a 2 goal lead. This is a disaster for us as we have struggled to overturn 1 goal deficits this season and have never come back from 2 down. Bradford trudge off at half time looking thoroughly dejected.

The second half starts and we are a team transformed. A well worked corner pulls one back and not long after we are level. The momentum is with us. This is it. Enter yet more Bradford fan idiocy. A moron in our end decides this is the point to throw a flare on the pitch. The game is stopped and all our momentum is lost. "Tosser" – literally!. You would think Bradford fans would know better. Sure enough we huff and puff and fail to exert any authority on the rest of the game. A draw won't be enough. Then in injury time, just to make the night complete, the ref awards a penalty to Crewe and we have lost. You just get nights like that sometimes.

"And I'm not that fond of Crewe".

To be fair, I do have a friend who is a Crewe fan. So I did go once as a Crewe fan. Leeds were in town so it was a good chance to sing "You're just a small town near Bradford". But I got some funny looks, sitting in the main stand. I should have gone behind the goal!

Chesterfield

I loved Chesterfield. A proper old-fashioned ground with some nearby proper old fashioned pubs selling great beer at a fair price. Add in the tourist attraction of the crooked spire and what more can you ask of your away day experience. They will be a very welcome addition back to the football league when they no doubt get promoted at the end of this season. I hope their new ground is worth a visit.

Needless to say, we lost this game, this being the 95/96 season. Our performance not being helped by Richard Liburd's red card. I loved Richard, he was my kind of player but he was definitely in the "Rolls Royce legs, Skoda brain" category. Can you say that now Skoda has improved?

Years later I was listening to Jermaine Jenas waffle on. I must have been bored? And you could have knocked me over with a feather when he revealed that our own Richard Liburd was his cousin and whilst at Bradford he had played a real father figure role for him. Remember Jenas was briefly Britain's most expensive teenager and the rumours were that the diamond earrings had gone to his head. Anyway Dickie Liburd was not much of a role model that day. Looking back through the programme I see Sean Dyche was playing. 168 appearances to that date for Chesterfield. Later to become a great manager in my view, capable of overachieving with a limited budget, which few of the top managers know how to do.

Rotherham

I first tried to go to Rotherham in 1991. I was on a week-long course in Sheffield and of course, itching to tick a ground off my list. My colleague was not a football fan, but he wasn't much of a drinker either, so when I offered him a session on the ale in Sheffield or a trip to Rotherham United he took the lesser of two evils. Pre internet and pre smartphones, information was pretty sparse on third tier games in those days. So we got all the way to Millmoor before we found out the game was off for a frozen pitch. "Never mind" I said. "We can go to Bradford tomorrow night. They have a cover for the pitch – it's guaranteed to be on". And off to the pub we went. The following night we drove up to Valley Parade only to find that the pitch cover was removed as normal, 2 hours before kick-off. It had then started to dump down with snow. So, of course the game was off. And we were off to the pub again.

Coming in to 1996, I still hadn't ticked Millmoor off the list. We were due to play Rotherham on 30th December 95, but of course , the game was postponed for bad weather. The match was rearranged for Tuesday 23rd January and I began to hatch a plan. By now it was becoming obvious that my days of gainful employment in Swindon were coming to an end. A big reorganisation (Downsizing, cull? – call it what you will!) meant I was going to be out of the job in a few months anyway. Liberated from guilt feelings I found myself a very tenuous reason for a business trip to Sheffield and the game was on and all on expenses. This was the season that Geoffrey Richmond had begun to pour money into the club, he talked ridiculously of premier league ambitions. Nobody believed him. But we were doing ok. Eighth in the league, level with Wrexham and only 1 point off Burnley for a play-off spot. Despite having Shaun Goater, Rotherham were poor that season and looked a good bet for relegation. Of course, we lost 2-0.

I've been back to the new ground. The improbably named New York stadium. It's not too bad. There are real pubs near the ground. I'm guessing land is cheap in Rotherham? We lost again. In fact, the old ground, Millmoor, is still standing and I believe they even host some football there. I wonder why they moved? Pat drove to meet us at the new ground and wandering back to the car in the dark stood ankle deep in horse shit. Police horses?. Could have done with that luck during the game.

Hull City

Coming into the final game of the 95/96 season, Bradford were sitting sixth, the last play-off place. This was unbelievable to me and Pat, as we seemed to have lost virtually every game we had been to that year!. In fact I have just added it up. we had been to 14 games together that season. We had won 1, drawn 2 and lost 11. A magical 5 points from 14 games. Somehow, even worse, the only win had been the first game we went to. It seemed an awful long time since we had won. I really am a bad jinx on my club. Here are the games:

Notts Co Away – Won 2-0
Swindon Away – Lost 4-1
Peterborough Away – Lost 3-1
Swansea Away – Lost 2-0
Chesterfield – Lost 2-1
Brentford Away – Lost 2-1
Bournemouth Away – Lost 3-1
Shrewsbury Away – Drew 1-1 (Hurray)
Bristol C Away A – Lost 2-1
Oxford Away – Lost 2-0
Wycombe Away – Lost 5-2
Bristol R Away – Lost 1-0
Walsall Away – Lost 2-1
Swindon Home – Drew 1-1

Still, a win at Hull would see us in the play offs. Hull were having a terrible year and went into the last game plumb bottom, 20 points off safety with a goal difference of minus 40. It had been all over for Hull that season for quite some time and attendances had suffered.

The Hull board came up with a cunning (cunningly stupid?) plan to earn extra revenue. Its only 70 miles from Bradford to Hull so they thought they would cash in by selling lots of tickets to Bradford fans. This took the form of giving the large home terrace to the away fans and the away terrace to the home fans. I can't imagine this would go down well anywhere, and add in the "Yorkshire derby" element, this always seemed a high risk strategy.

This was the early days of the internet. But by 1996 lots of chat rooms were going and it was obvious from the chatter that this was going to be a troubled game. Nevertheless Pat and I were not going to miss this one. Its over 200 miles and nearly 5 hours to Hull from Swindon but away we went. We could tell it was going to be an "interesting" day as we parked up. Parking next to us were some Stoke City fans (no colours but a Stoke City pendant in the back of the car which they were now taking down and putting in the glove box). "Hi, what are you doing here" we asked, naively assuming they were ground hunters or similar. "We are here for the bother" they said as they waltzed off looking for a pub. Great.

We headed to a different pub! We got talking to some Hull fans and it was all very friendly. We discussed Wayne Jacobs, ex Hull now playing for Bradford. An odd player, he looked distinctly average (to us) in the third tier, not good, not bad, just average, but he stayed with Bradford all the way for 2 seasons in the premier league and managed to look just as average in the Prem! I said they could have him back if they let us win – What do I know!

In an absolute roller coaster of a game Hull go 1-0 up and 2-1 up before Bradford equalise in the 25th minute – all bracketed by multiple pitch invasions, both Hull and Bradford fans, idiots. Credit to the police who did a great job of keeping the fans in the stand from about the 30 minute mark onwards. Bradford won 3-2 and we are in the play offs. An outcome that had looked unlikely for most of the season. Now we just had to get back to the car. The police had done an excellent job inside the ground but outside was a different matter. There were fights everywhere. At one point Pat and I found ourselves walking through someone's back garden to avoid all the skirmishes. Eventually we did make it back to the car. Inevitably the league launched an enquiry into the events of the day. I can't remember what the enquiry found, but this has not happened again on my travels.

We went back to the Ring O Bells in Shipley, a well known Bradford fans pub and after a couple of celebratory drinks a van full of Bradford lads turned up. One had had his ear half bitten off in the aftermath. But he wasn't letting that spoil his day and it certainly wasn't stopping him having some more beers.

Not Blackpool

If there was one away game I missed, that I really wish I could go back and see it would be Blackpool away. Play off second leg. May 1996. I had booked a last minute cheap break to Sorrento which was bad planning when I realised this would mean I couldn't go to the game. But then Bradford lost the first leg at home 2-0. So, no harm done. A hell of a drive from Swindon to see us meekly lose and fail in our promotion bid. I was better off on holiday, or so I thought.

Of course, there is always hope. I remember on the evening of the game, sitting in a restaurant in Southern Italy and thinking "Its half time, If we've scored one by now there is still hope". In 1996 there are no smart phones or internet cafes and a phone call home is very expensive. I write this thought off. I'm not paying £3 to find out we have lost. I have done my research though. There was a newsagents in Sorrento that stocked English newspapers. They came over with the tourists so tended to arrive at about 11.30. I had overdone the alcohol a bit, the night before so I was nursing a bit of a hangover when I popped in the following morning. The newspapers were very expensive so the trick was to quickly find the results page and read the score before the owner shouts at you.

I couldn't believe my eyes. 3-0, we had won 3-0 away from home, overturning the deficit. We were going to Wembley. Bradford at Wembley! It had never happened before. I went and bought myself an orange Solero (great for hangovers) and went back to my room to put on my Bradford shirt. Incredible. Now it is time for the £3 phone home. Pat's mum will pop down to Valley Parade and get the tickets. I think she bought about 15 in the end. It's all sorted!

Realistically there's probably only two other away games I really regret that I missed.

Aston Villa away to secure a League Cup final place. Instead I was sat in my dressing gown at home sipping a gin and tonic (or possibly gulping?) and nervously checking the BBC website updates. We make it to the final whistle and the challenge is on to get tickets.

The very same season, Burton away to overturn another play off first leg deficit. But this time I somehow wasn't nervous at all. Instead I was playing football in the back garden with my boys and listening in on DAB radio. I don't know why I wasn't nervous at all that time. Sometimes you seem to just know. No worries about getting tickets for this Wembley trip!

Sheff Utd and QPR

In the summer following our play-off victory, Pat and I had the summer off. We were both waiting to get made redundant. It was certainly very nice getting paid not to work but we knew it would end. Pat was off back to Oxford to do teacher training and I would need a new job. I took the opportunity to "get fit". I was still young enough to think that if only I could get fit enough I would be as good as the guys I watched – Ha.

One day in the mid-summer heat Pat and I played tennis. Neither of us could serve very well so we ground each other into the dirt. Eventually giving up at 7-7 I think through heat exhaustion. So July sees us back in Bradford for a couple of pre-season friendlies at Guiseley and Thackley with Bobby Mimms on trial I remember at Guiseley – he didn't sign. With my new trim body we are back in the second tier. I hope the players have done as much training as I have!

We were well off the pace in our first games back in the second tier, with players like Eric Regtop (sorry Eric but 8 games and 1 goal for our main striker was less than we hoped for, you did better at your next club so maybe it wasn't your fault?) who were just not good enough for this level. So games like Sheff U away did not hold out much hope. It was only September but we had already lost home and away to them in the league cup. On my way from Swindon up to Sheffield I called in to Solihull to see my old British Gas boss Ken. He decided he would come with me to Sheffield. I'm good at dragging people to games! We lost again 3-0 and that is all I remember. I haven't been back.

On to QPR. "Bradford have lost all their previous three matches at Loftus Road and have yet to score a goal" gloated the programme. Well that is promising. It's October and we are third bottom but not yet adrift. I'm not working as I am still waiting to get made redundant so I have had a leisurely day looking round the science museum and then on to the natural history museum where I saw (I kid you not), a kamarasaurus. An omen for our manager? Actually it is spelt camarasaurus.   Maybe there is a loophole? No such luck. We lose 1-0, still not a single goal at Loftus Road.

A few years later in April 1999, with promotion beckoning, I returned to Loftus Road. By now we are playing fans games first and we are playing the Rangers fans in the park with the delightful setting of wormwood scrubs in the background. Pats brother Eddie scores a worldie with a bicycle kick. That must be the omen. And it is. We finally break our duck and go on to win the real game 3-1. Eddie now tells me he thinks he hit the crossbar with that shot but I prefer to think he scored. Anyway we won.

Charlton

Bradfords early days back in the second tier continued to be challenging. Weak at the back and toothless up front is never a great recipe. The step up was proving a difficult one to make. By 23rd November we were third bottom on 17 points from 19 games. Away at Charlton did not look a promising place to turn form around, but early signings such as Chris Waddle did show that our chairman had some depth to his pocket and his ambition. Football is a brutal world and with the benefit of hindsight I can tell you that not one of the players who turned out for us that day would survive 3 years to our opening premiership game. One guy who certainly could have made it was Mark Schwarzer, but he went on to greater things elsewhere.

Schwarzer was a completely unknown entity to us that lunchtime as we sat in the pub, the Watermans Arms, discussing our bleak prospects. The pub was nice enough, with lots of Charlton memorabilia and still an excited new buzz to it as it was not long since they had returned to the Valley after a long exile. As we chatted away we mentioned that our current keeper, Jon Gould wasn't up to the task, but neither were most of the other players. The day before, we had signed Schwarzer from Kaiserslautern where he had only made 4 appearances so he wasn't setting our world on fire. Again, what did I know.

Schwarzer put in one of the best goalkeeping performances I have ever seen in a City shirt as we surprised Charlton and ourselves with a 2-0 win. For once, I was not alone in my assessment of a player and the scouts appeared quickly. Schwarzer only played 13 games for us before moving on up to premiership Middlesbrough. For me he is the best Bradford keeper I have ever seen. That definitely includes Jordan Pickford by the way.

Grimsby

We might have found a gem of a keeper but we were still bobbing around the bottom of the table as we headed to Grimsby the following month. December 21st possibly doesn't show Grimsby at its finest. Grimsby actually play in nearby Cleethorpes and as you head along a completely deserted dual carriageway (in December 96) you see brown tourist signs darkly warning "Beware tourist traffic likely". Maybe it is busier in summer? There wasn't a car to be seen!

The pubs were pretty awful back then in Grimsby but it was worth it for the fish and chips. You have to go to Grimsby for the fish and chips. The size of the fish I got. I have seen smaller submarines! We ground out a stodgy 1-1 draw and continued to hope we might survive in this league.

Pat and I tried to go back in 2003. Again a Xmas game. We got all the way to Grimsby where we reprised our visit to the "Leaking Boot". As I said, not a great pub but welcoming to away fans. It was a huge pub and they had a separate room for away fans, but this time we were all alone. Still not great! A local came over and said "what are you doing here" – Oh no, trouble? "How do you mean?" we ask. "The games been called off". Great, nothing on the radio about that. We drove to a local multiplex and watched Lord of the Rings – the two towers instead. I'm sure it was more entertaining!

On the way home we saw a man standing on the motorway bridge getting ready to jump off so we pulled over and called the police. The wonders of modern technology. He didn't jump so hopefully we helped save him that day.

Everton

Goodison Park is a ground I know very well. I lived within earshot of the ground for two years whilst at University in Liverpool and have been to countless games there. I have been in all four sides. It is a done deal for me. Fortunately, as it is soon to be demolished for what looks (for once) to be a much better ground in a better location. If you are in the main stand I do hope you are not scared of heights as I have never been in a ground with such vertiginous seats. Maybe take a rope and strap yourself in? If you are in the Bullens road, good luck, you will see some of the game but you will probably have a blocked view unless you are near the front.

I have only seen Bradford play there once. But what a game. As long as you are not a toffee. January 97 and second tier Bradford are away to premier Everton in the 4th round of the FA Cup. We were housed in the lower tier of the Bullens road and from where I was stood, if the ball was kicked above head high, you couldn't see it until it came back down. The first half was uneventful but the first 14 minutes of the second half certainly delivered. Bradford scored once, then Chris Waddle pounced on the ball and spotted Southhall off his line. In my memory, Waddle was by the halfway line, but YouTube suggests it was more like 35 yards out. He aims to chip the keeper, the ball goes up into the sky and we lose sight of it thanks to the roof of the upper tier. Suddenly the ball appears in the back of the net. Before we can even get our breath back from our giddy celebrations, Everton have scored, and before we have chance to panic, Bradford have scored again. In a crazy 14 minutes at the start of the second half Bradford are 3-1 up away at Everton. The match calms down and the rest of the half is good steady stuff, until in the 90th minute, Everton score, but it's too little, too late and we are through 3-2 away at Everton. Amazing.

We head back to the car in Stanley Park and I grab a Bakewell tart in triumph. "Piece of cake!" I say and off we drive.

Stockport

10th January 1998. It had been a tumultuous week for Bradford. Lying in mid table, Bradford had chosen this week as the right time to part company with Chris Kamara. Chris is a legend at Bradford both as a player and a manager but the general feeling was that he had taken us as far as he could and our chairman wanted more. So within the club and its fanbase there wasn't all that much surprise, but an element of the media seized on this story with a righteous froth and zeal. Chris was one of the few non white managers at the time and a fair effort was made by sections of the media to write this story as pure racism. Apparently, he had lost his job because of his skin colour. Bless him, Chris put this story right as soon as he could. David Mellor (remember him?) had specifically called our chairman racist to the point at which Geoffrey had written to demand Mellors removal from the football task force. When our local paper talked to Chris he was asked if the sacking was racially motivated and he said, "Yeah, I walked into Geoffrey's office and he said "Chris, I've been working with you for a bit over 2 years now and I've just realised you're not white. You're fired." Of course it wasn't racist. Chris is a legend, surely the best pundit ever to appear on Sky?.

We had appointed Paul Jewell as caretaker manager and this was his first game so I was keen to see how it went. I had just moved to Manchester and was planning my trip. It turned out my local geography was not that great. I would get the train from Manchester to Stockport. Blimey it's the main line train to London. How far away is Stockport? I'd better leave plenty of time. So on the day I got on the inter-city special and about 4 minutes later, got off in Stockport. I was miles early. It's about a 10 minute walk from there to the ground. Leaving me plenty of time to sample the joys of Edgeley. Edgeley is a less affluent part of Stockport, and for football grounds, so much the better. There was a plethora of pubs, selling very cheap beer. I think one of the Sam Smiths pubs I visited was doing a £1 a pint. Tremendous value.

I have been back a fair few times and whilst Edgeley remains its parsimonious self, Stockport County do not follow this philosophy. The season ticket prices are twice that at Bradford. And the pies! £5.50 for a pie! In Edgeley! Anyway, back to the football.

The day started well , as I got to touch the ball during warm up. I always take this as a good sign. It always surprises me how little people pay attention in warm ups. Well trained men are kicking the ball as hard as they can, approximately straight at you if you are stood behind the goal. Sure enough, not for the last time. A parent had sat his young boy on a barrier, facing away from the goal. A full blooded wayward shot came in and knocked him splat onto the ground. The player came over mortified. But on this occasion, no harm done.

All the omens were good, and sure enough we won 2-1. The team needed major surgery to have a chance of making the premier league, but the seeds were sown.

Eric Nixon was in goal for Stockport. A fine keeper I am sure. And he seems a nice lad. He has done well pretty much everywhere he has been. Except Bradford. Eric came to Bradford on a short term loan in 1986 for 3 games and back again in 96 for 12 games. My memory tells me he let in 4 goals every time I saw him play!. In fact in 86, he let in 4, 2 and 3 in his 3 goal spell. I don't remember his 96 spell that well, but it can't have been good the way we were teasing each other. Great guy!.

I have also been to Stockport to watch a Rugby Union game. It really confirmed all my prejudices about the sport. My mate Paul

(Man City fan) had some season tickets so off we went for a Friday night game, Sale Sharks vs someone? I just don't get it. There are some games that actually make good spectator sports and the rest are presumably mostly about the atmosphere? We stood at one end of the ground and there would be a massive ruck at the other end and eventually the ref would intervene. Not my cup of tea.

Of the sports I have seen live I would count only three as actually fully watchable live: Football (of course), Greyhounds and NFL (helped by having big screen replays).

Sports I have been to, but I just think work better on TV. Rugby, Horse Racing, Motorsport, Cycling (!) Golf and sadly Cricket. I love cricket, but let's face it. If you want to see the game you get a much better view on TV. Going is more of a summer picnic event with a chance of some drunken excitement towards the end of the day. A Caribbean winter tour with England is definitely in my retirement plans, but a county game on a cold Wednesday is only for those who like solitude.

Southend and Bury

Another pair of clubs now struggling in non-league.

Bury first. At least Bury are now playing and have their own ground back. It looked bad for a while. I used to love Bury away. Not far, great pubs, friendly people. I remember the Rose and Crown on Manchester Old Road much clearer than I remember the games. Cracking pub. I took my wife once in our early days. It was a freezing cold day and she didn't know what to expect. Her memory of the day is being surrounded by huge Bradford lads radiating warmth. I'm not clear that she saw any of the game.

She doesn't come now. My last visit was an unusual affair. In early 2016 Bury were struggling for cash and drew a "plum" tie, home to Bradford in the FA Cup. You can't really tell in the photo below but to capitalise on the number of Bradford fans who would make the quick trip over the pennines, Bury gave us both ends. It would have been very strange if we had scored! The game ended 0-0.

In 2024, Southend are not that far off a return to the league but they have had troubled times of late. I have a mate that lives in Southend so it would be good to have an excuse to go back. I went in 1997 and we drew 1-1. I think we had a walk to the "front" and got some chips. It was April but it felt more like January, so not very "sea sidey".

One constant of my poor memory of these days is that all my mates remember the goals better than I do. I remember the pubs and the journey and the goal celebrations. Pat assures me our Brazilian striker (I kid you not) Edinho scored for us that day against Southend. Edinho remains a fan favourite and is still often seen at the ground. He was a bit too fond of the "dark arts" for my taste but each to their own.

Ipswich

I first visited Ipswich in 1994. I found myself in town on a Tuesday night for a work trip to visit Eastern Electricity. Bolton were playing in the Coca Cola Cup and so it was a chance for another ground. I had no hotel booked for the night so I popped into the tourist information centre to sort one and while I was getting fixed up they asked me what I would do with the evening. I mentioned I would pop along to the football and they said they could do me a ticket for that as well. I thought nothing more of it and bought a ticket for the match as well. I turned up at Portman road 2 hours later and wandered up to find my seat. The tourist information centre must have had a block of about 500 tickets at their disposal that night and how many do you think they sold? – That's right, one. It was a bit lonely but I had a great view. I bet everybody thought I was a steward.

Of course I needed to return to see Bradford. My chance came in January 1998. I had started a new job which involved a fair few London trips. In my northern mind Ipswich is close to London, so I had arranged to kip at my mate Adams house in Clapham, South London. I pestered him and he agreed to drive us to Ipswich. He's a northerner too (although totally acclimatised to London these days). I think he must have been suffering Northern geography too when he agreed. Its nearly a 2.5 hour drive from Clapham to Ipswich. What a journey. All I can do is apologise. Sorry Adam. Anyway I know better for next time.

The game itself was the first time (I think) that I had sat high up in the main stand. I do prefer to stand and this does tend to be behind the goal. And generally I stand reasonably low down. This tends to make football a really visceral experience without affording a great opportunity to analyse the tactics of the two teams. This suits me best. I find that when discussing (and especially writing about) football, or pop music or fine wine there does to my mind seem to be an awful lot of "cows' testicles" written:

This wine tastes of elderflower with hits of red cabbage and cigar box, hmm – I just think it's a nice red wine. You know the type. Kalvin Philipps ran the midfield with stern majesty - hmm – I didn't think he touched the ball and he still got a yellow.. And so on. Anyway, that night was the first time, after over a decade of football watching that I could really "see" the formations swirl around the pitch rather than just watch the players huff and puff. Bradford played a very well drilled two banks of four. It didn't really add to my enjoyment so I am still behind the goal to this day.

Norwich

It is only right to follow Ipswich with Norwich. Two teams, 45 miles apart that still think they are playing a "local" derby. That's East Anglia for you I suppose. I once did some work in Lowestoft and was told the nearest motorway was in Holland! Norwich is just a long way away from anywhere. And in some respects all the better for it. It is a lovely city, but it takes some getting to. In 1989 I made an "interesting" choice to catch the Liverpool supporters coach to Norwich. Nearing the end of the season Norwich were second, behind Arsenal and Liverpool were third so it was a big game. I think we set off at 6.30. My biggest memory of the day was arriving at the ground to be frisked. For some reason I was frisked by a female PC and she said (titter ye not) "what's this in your pocket". To which all her male colleagues fell about laughing. I don't know if this was their usual routine for entertainment but it has stuck with me. It was my car keys by the way.

It is always a fools game to predict the future but the first page of the programme got it splendidly wrong that day. The programme felt the need to start with a comment section on the "state of the game" and chose 3 things:

1. Referees – Apparently it's a bad thing for referees to want to be professional. I think they meant full time? How can it not be better for a referee to be full time so he can focus on fitness and the rules? Refs eventually turned full time in 2001 so ***it took 12 years to be wrong.***
2. Wembley has campaigned for a refurb so we don't have to knock it down. It would be a disaster for the game to knock it down and rebuild. "It isn't the concrete that matters" – hmmm. As we know, Wembley was demolished in 2002 so ***it took 13 years to be wrong.***
3. Newport County were going out of business, this would be very sad (agreed) and it is now inevitable. Newport were saved by 12 fine upstanding chaps less than a month later. OK – it took them 25 years to get back in the league, but hey, they are still going!

I wish I'd got a few more of these comment pages – genius.

I got to tick Norwich off my list property with Bradford in 1998. I was staying at my mate Jem's house near Cambridge. Norwich really is a long way from anywhere and I had totally underestimated the drive time. It ended up taking nearly 2 hours, and I thought I was nearly there! I only just made it for kick off. Bradford won an entertaining game 3-2. This obviously didn't go down too well with the locals and I got "bodied" walking through the car park on the way out (I must have been smiling?). Definite yellow card ref! No intention of playing the ball!

Watford and Lincoln

I don't know what it's like supporting your team. For me supporting Bradford you tend to go into each new season with a vague hope that things might work out well, but generally no great confidence. The start of season 98/99 was different. We had recruited with real tangible ambition. We expected to do well. The squad looked great. On paper. But would it be "great on paper, crap on grass" as Brian Clough didn't quite say. The answer was that it really took these players a fair few games to gel. So it was I met up with Pat and Eddie at Watford in great hope only to see us narrowly fall 1-0.

Three days later, Bradford are at Lincoln in the league cup. Having underwhelmed the previous week with a 1-1 draw at home against unfancied Lincoln. Well, I had to go. Its midweek and it's a fair old drive from Manchester. Klaas is now "loved up" as they say, having met a kiwi girl who turns out to be "the one". He had always wanted to emigrate to New Zealand so there was an inevitability about this. I was his best man in Queenstown in 2001 and the Klaas years had gone. Klaas remains happily married in New Zealand. Good lad. Pat is still down south so that's not working either.

So I end up going on my own. I have one clear memory for the night. I had bought fish and chips. Not a patch on the Grimsby offering. When I finished them I walked around the entire ground looking for a bin. No bin, so I asked a policeman. "No bins mate, bomb threat" – (Really?), "Just chuck it on the floor!". We managed to get through the game without a terrorist explosion and we crawled over the line 1-0. The season was yet to ignite. But at least the bins hadn't?

I had an "interesting" company car at the time. I had inherited it from a senior manager who had then been "asked to leave". It was a green BMW 2.8i Coupe, with yellow leather seats. A lovely car to drive but an interesting colour scheme. A comfortable drive home but still nearly 1 am by the time I got home, so straight to bed. As I fell asleep I heard a funny noise but really couldn't be bothered to investigate. In the morning it turned out that the local "lad" had chosen this night to break into my car. Strange hobby, he was going round all the local cars one by one. There was nothing inside to steal so I think he just did it to prove he could, no damage!

No more new grounds for me that season, but much better, a final game of the season with the possibility of promotion to the promised land of the premier league.

Wolves

Molineux is a ground I've visited many times. The first time was a quick trip up the road whilst I lived in Solihull. April 1991 to see Wolves play Swindon. Wolves had an outside chance of the playoffs (as usual) and Swindon, managed by Glenn Hoddle, were in a relegation fight. Wolves were a good value watch at that time with Steve Bull leading the line for Wolves with 27 goals so far that season. Just behind Millwall's Teddy Sheringham as the league's top scorer. Wolves lost 2-1 to presage the unlikely rise of Swindon Town to the premier league "Up where we belong" as the Swindon Bugle was later to record – somewhat unwisely. My biggest memory of the night was all the building work. Sir Jack Hayward bought the club for £2.1m in 1990 with the pledge to transform Molineux. Over the next three years, all but the John Ireland Stand was rebuilt, as Molineux was transformed at a cost of £20m. That was a LOT of money back then.

I returned twice in the late 90's to see the fruits of this investment. First in August 1996 to see newly promoted Bradford take on a wolves team still lead by Steve Bull. The game is most memorable for the fact that our keeper Jon Gould got injured and had to go off. Only 2 subs back then and we had no reserve keeper on the bench so Carl Shutt our 5 foot 11 inch striker volunteered. At one point facing a shot he controlled the ball beautifully on the line and dribbled to the edge of the area before remembering he was the keeper. Those were the days. In truth we were way off the pace in the early days of promotion and as they say we were lucky to get nil. The game ending 1-0 to Wolves.

My last visit to date was on 9th May 1999. Another date etched into the memories of Bradford fans. At this point I had never had a season ticket for Bradford, it just wasn't necessary, and I mostly went to away games which never sold out. So when the final game of the 98/99 season arrived away at Wolves, win and you are promoted to the premier league. My chances of getting a ticket were zero. Pat to the rescue. "We can get tickets in the Main stand – fancy it?" You bet I did. I have to say how lovely the Wolves fans were. If you are just pleasant and honest, most football fans are actually really nice people.

I encourage you to watch the game, it's on YouTube. For once in my lifetime, this season Bradford were playing beautiful cultured football. Wolves were much more direct and physical and also playing with a real chance of a play-off spot themselves . So by no means a push over. In a fast paced game Bradford took a 3-1 lead and with 15 minutes to go ex Bradford legend Dean Richards concedes a penalty – The promised land beckons. Up steps Peter Beagrie, star of the season. The goalkeeper saves and at the same time news comes through that Ipswich are 4-1 up, so we really have to win. Still, no worries right? Only 15 minutes to go and 3-1 up. Of course up the other end pops in

Paul Simpson and its 3-2. By now all the Wolves fans around us know we are Bradford fans having to sit in the wrong end. Wolves get a free kick and hit the post. Here began the inspiration for the excellent Bradford fanzine "Width of a Post". You could clearly hear the ping of the ball as it whacked back off the woodwork.

"You must be shitting yourselves" sing the Wolves fans. Really, they are not wrong. After an eternity the game finally ends and we are up into the premier league. We shake hands with the Wolves fans who seem genuinely pleased for us. I really will have to get a season ticket.

In the late 80's I started reading the Independent newspaper, A habit now long gone. I was still buying it sporadically in the 90's as internet coverage of Bradford was still sparse, mostly confined to chat room mutter. I started to develop a distinct dislike of Patrick Barclay during these years. The Guardian, Independent and Observers' "top football writer" and all round football snob. Before the game at Wolves Barclay chose fit to express his opinion that he hoped Ipswich would get promoted, this fine old institution would surely grace the premier league more than a toiling Bradford who perennially belonged to the lower leagues. Really?

I had assumed that Trent Crimm in the occasionally excellent Ted Lasso was modelled on Barclay, but apparently not. More of Barclay later but I soon got feedback that the average football fans view was much more accommodating of our imminent premier league arrival.

After the game I returned home. At the time I was living in what we euphemistically (optimistically?) called Chorlton Borders. A suburb of Manchester actually called Whalley Range if you know Manchester. About a mile and a half walk from Old Trafford. Buzzing from the game and the thought of actually being at Old

Trafford and all the other grounds next season I certainly wasn't going to settle down to a cup of tea and an early night. So, on goes the Bradford top and a walk to Chorlton to sample the fine pubs in the area. I lost count of the number of cars speeding past who tooted their horn in celebration when they saw my Bradford top. Football fans in general, know their shirts and know when an achievement is made and how to celebrate it. What a day!

So that's three sides of the Wolves ground done, I must go back one day and do the Stan Cullis stand and I will be complete.

Liverpool

I've been to Anfield more than fifty times, but the proper away day experience came in November 99. It was my first time back in a decade and the first time I had ever driven to the ground. It was a bus or a walk while I lived in Liverpool. We arrived quite late as I had drastically underestimated the impact of the 90's financial boom on traffic levels in Liverpool. Back in the 80's they used to call Liverpool the city without a rush hour. That's certainly not true any more. So we finally got within a mile or so of the ground and parked up. "Fiver to look after your car mate" shouted some scally appearing from nowhere. "No thanks", I shouted back as we'd already set off for the ground. "It's a company car, do what you want!". He looked a bit puzzled and then moved on to find someone else to scam. The car was fine when we got back to it.

I went with my mate Surish, a Liverpool fan. Maybe I'm a terrible friend? Always dragging people into the Bradford end to watch football? I think he was just pleased to get to go. By then it was getting hard to get tickets for the big clubs. And he did get a free lift to the game. Anyway, he left happy.

The game started well, with Dean Windass volleying a superb goal for us to take a surprise lead. But it didn't last. We lost 3-1. Little did we know at that stage that the return leg at valley parade, the last game of the season, would be such a crucial game. But that's a different story.

That was not quite Anfield complete for me. I still had one stand left to do. That had to wait until November 2021. And my younger self would be turning in his grave, if that sort of analogy is even possible. As a student I had often stood on the kop moaning about the gradual tide of big money ruining the spirit of the game. The "prawn sandwich brigade" who came to the game as if it was a theatre production to be enjoyed from a distance, not a rousing rabble intent on having their say and hopeful to have their sway on the opposition or on the ref. I would have been unsurprised but also appalled at how much this tide of money has impacted on the football experience. Now I was about to see it first-hand.

In 2021 I was working as the MD of a company that was building refuelling stations for hydrogen cars and this was very much flavour of the month at that time. A string of big and rich companies came to talk to us as they all wanted to assess whether there was a business here for them. One of them happened to ask about football during the small talk and it soon became clear I was dead keen. So at the end of the meeting they asked me if I wanted "a few tickets" for the Liverpool game that weekend. These few tickets turned out to be, pretty much the most expensive executive box you can buy at Anfield. Only my youngest, Eddie was living at home so I accepted three tickets and off my wife, Eddie and I went. The tickets came complete with a parking space actually inside the Shankly gates. At the time I was (obviously) driving a hydrogen car and this looked very exclusive and expensive, complete with tinted rear windows, I think a lot of people thought I was chauffeuring a celebrity or a football person and we got a lot of curious looks as we drove in through the gates. I already felt a million dollars, but then we are whisked away with a champagne reception and taken straight for a four course meal. In the box.

At the top of the main stand. Pretty much by the centre circle as you can see from the picture I took. And the bonus was that this ticked off the fourth side of the ground for me. I don't know what this day was, but it certainly didn't feel like football as I know it. It was a cold November day but we were in heated luxury and if we chose to venture out to watch the game, blankets were provided. Occasionally people below us in the stand would look up to see if they could spot anyone famous. At half time we are ushered back in for yet more food – artisan pie and posh mushy peas. For some foolish reason Southampton had turned up intent on playing attacking football and they were brushed aside 4-0. I have to say that for a 4-0 win the atmosphere was distinctly flat. If that was football I wouldn't bother going. I hate to think how much it cost.

Man Utd

Memories play tricks on you. My memory is that we played Manchester United four times in the two premier league years and we lost 4-0 every time. In fact, checking the records its slightly worse than that. 4-0, 4-0, 6-0, 3-0. Maybe we were slightly improving there at the end? My trip to Old Trafford was on Boxing day 1999. I was living in Chorlton at the time so at most a two mile walk to the ground. Getting tickets had been a challenge. Despite now having a season ticket, it was still a case of queuing. Anticipation of this game was huge. Man U being the dominant force at the time. I drove over to Bradford to get a ticket and the queue was very long, it didn't look promising. Bradford are really not set up for this sort of thing. Probably three kiosks open to sell 3,000 tickets. I joined the queue with a book and read for about an hour as we steadily shuffled forward. I was stressing all the time that they would sell out just before it was my turn. I eventually got to the front and bought two tickets (mine and Pats season tickets).

Pat couldn't go as it was boxing day so I took my mate Chris who isn't a football fan at all but fancied a day out, especially if the opportunity for a drink was involved. "Shall we cycle" said Chris. "Are you mad, have you ever seen a crowd of 70,000 football fans". He agreed later that cycling would have been a challenging adventure. As a side note, we now have "safe cycle parking" at Valley Parade. Crowds are 15,000 to 20,000 but even so I don't know who would want to cycle through that. Especially when you add "Bradford drivers" and Manningham Lane to the mix. I guess that's modern traffic planners for you? I love cycling, but I wouldn't cycle to a game.

In our first season in the premier league we were "plucky contenders" and I always felt we had an outside chance of doing something. Prior to the game a Man U fan at work was telling me how we were going to get battered. I said, "Give me a 3 goal head start and put a tenner on it". All went to plan for a very long time. Until the 75th minute in fact. 0-0 with 15 minutes to go. I've won a tenner here I'm thinking. And more importantly I've won the bragging rights. Oh dear. First Quinton Fortune (remember him? No, not really), Then Yorke, Cole and finally Keane. It was like they were queuing up for shooting practice. We lost 4-0 and I lost the bet.

Old Trafford is another of the grounds I've been in all 4 sides of. I feel I've done the lot. I've sat in the main stand with the Man U fans so I can taunt Leeds. Man U won 2-0. I've sat with the prawn sandwich brigade at a European Cup night (3-3 vs Spartak Moscow, what a game). That night was prime prawn sandwich. A mate (Spurs fan) who also worked in the energy industry unexpectedly came by his company's corporate tickets. Four executive seats and a free nosh up with one catch. You had to work in the energy industry as Gareth would have to write a report on who he took (for the tax man?). So off we go, Gareth (Spurs), Paul (Man City), Me (Bradford) and Gareth's mate (Never met him before). So we are sat having a fine meal before the game and I turn to Gareth's mate "Well, I hope you are a Man U fan?". "Absolutely not!" he replied. Utter prawn sandwich. What would Roy Keane say?

My last trip was to tick off the Stretford End. We got tickets for England v N Macedonia. 7-0. And a thoroughly enjoyable summer evening. I am a bit sad that I never stood on the Stretford end. But there is at least a small amount of safe standing there now. We were in the seats, a little cramped but I have had a lot worse.

You hear a lot of moaning from a section of Man U fans about how their ground is embarrassing and dilapidated. I must admit, I really liked it. It's a proper old fashioned ground with a good atmosphere. I far preferred it to modern Wembley. Yes the seats are a bit tight – so stand up! Yes the roof leaks, but that is because it is raining, wear a coat!. I didn't try the pies but now that Media City has been developed just over the footbridge in Salford Quays there is a great range of eating and drinking options as well. Yes, I like Old Trafford. It was even relatively straight forward driving home. With a handy Multi Storey in Salford Quays.

Spurs and Arsenal

I didn't get to as many away grounds as I might have liked, during the premier league years (1999 – 2001) as I got married in 2000. I was keen to see most of the home games, so away games were a challenge as I didn't want an early divorce. But I was definitely going to tick off Spurs and Arsenal. At this stage I was leaving Chelsea as I thought it would be nice to finish the 92 at my dads teams ground (I am not sure I had thought this through).

Tottenham Hotspur
F.A. Carling Premiership
SPURS vs BRADFORD CITY
Saturday   4 MAR 2000   3.00 p.m
BLOCK ROW SEAT PRICE
  37   11   154   £24.00
SOUTH LOWER G/WAY37 AWAY SUPPORTER

Bradford City FC

I missed Arsenal in the first season. In the second season it was a Tuesday night in January. By this time it was pretty obvious that this would be our last season in the premier league so I had to go. Pat was living in Aylesbury at the time, so I manoeuvred a work trip to take me down there and we got the train into London. From memory I think we played ok, but we lost 2-0. The writing was on the wall. It was great to have seen the old Highbury first hand. The queue for the tube afterwards was immense but we got home. I haven't been to the new Arsenal ground though I have seen it from high up on the hill at Alexander Palace. It looks pretty good. If we get a game there, next time I will walk back to Euston.

A better experience in some ways was Spurs. £24 to get in as you can see, which I thought was a bit steep back then. But it went up to £28 the next season. That's inflation. Still with first season optimism we visited in March 2000. We were struggling but not doomed. Spurs away was a bit of a free hit in the relegation fight as you don't budget to get any points. A Saturday in London and Pat can't make it so I turn to my long suffering mate Adam. At this point I am not so sure who Adam supports. He started off a Manchester lad supporting Man U. Indeed, he took me to watch Man U play West Ham a very long time ago. I don't remember much about the game but I do remember getting back to the old car park and turning on the radio to hear James Alexander Gordon intone in his familiar style – Bradford City 4…….Swansea City,,,,,,, 6.

Anyway, by now Adam is living in London and has switched allegiance to Arsenal, although he denies this now. So he is up for a shout at Spurs fans. Spurs take an early lead, but just before half time Jamie Lawrence pops in an equalizer and that's the way it stayed. A valuable point in the relegation battle. Adam is now a Fulham season ticket holder. Some people are so fickle. I did once tell Adam that of all my mates he was the one I most expected to get divorced. I think he took it well. He is currently on wife number two. Maybe she shouldn't read this? She told me recently that she was watching "Welcome to Wrexham" season 1 but she didn't know if they were going to get promoted. So I suspect there is not much chance of her getting this far in the book?

I recently visited the new Spurs stadium. For an NFL game as son number 1 is a Jacksonville Jags fan. Let's be honest it is a truly magnificent stadium and the acoustics are phenomenal , But…

I couldn't do that every week. First pass a line of stewards. "Sorry you can't take a rucksack in here". I had cycled to Warrington to catch the train to London. "I tell you what, I will empty my rucksack, put all my things in my pocket and fold up my rucksack, happy?" "Absolutely mate. I'm a Stokie. I think these rules are stupid. They want you to pay a tenner to store the rucksack". With a happy handshake we wander off to ticket check (electronic via complex App where you have to find the QR code). Then through an X Ray machine. Then through another ticket check. Finally, into the ground. We buy some overpriced lager. "I know the menu says craft beer but we don't have any". "Anywhere" I check. "Yep anywhere". Then off to our seats. At least you can drink in front of NFL. We are behind the goal near the top. It's a long steep climb but the views are magnificent. And it was loud. It was so loud that the Jags actually fumbled two plays as they couldn't hear what the quarterback was saying. I don't think they get noise like that in many of the NFL games back home. The jags won so it was a great day. But then you have to get back home. It's a 2 mile walk to the nearest tube and when you get there everyone else is queuing. I reckon around 30,000 people. We gave up and walked South, as we had plenty of time. Eventually making it to Euston over 2 hours after final whistle. A great stadium, but I couldn't do that 19 times a season.

I can't count Spurs new ground as I haven't seen "soccer" there, just NFL. But would it actually count anyway? The new ground is essentially built in the car park of the old ground and there is overlap of the stands. Other ground redevelopments like Molineux and Valley Parade have moved the pitch, so when does it actually become a new ground? I did have some online debate about this (silly me) and the justification for it being a new ground is that it has moved a bit and changed its name. I am not sure that if we moved valley parade to the car park and called it say the University of Bradford stadium that would be enough for me. If Bradford ever get to play a game at the Tottenham Hotspur Stadium I will have to decide.

Coventry

19th May 2001. Bradford had been relegated for some time by now but this was to be our last game in the premier league (ever?) so not to be missed. Coventry City were also well relegated as were Manchester City. Some fun to be had at the end of a long and miserable season perhaps.

This was my third and last visit to Highfield Road. My first was in 1990. Still fresh in my Solihull job, Liverpool were in town and about to be crowned league champions. As it happens for the last time in a long time, so I thought I would wander along. "GFGHGH's a shit hole I wanna go home" sing the away fans at most grounds these days. There is no doubt that the song was made for Coventry City centre in the early 90's. Maybe it has improved?, but actually the area around Highfield Road was delightfully pleasant park land. Off I go with the certainty of youth wandering up to the ground with no ticket. (Ah the 90's!). "Want a ticket" shouts someone, inevitably. "Yes please". It's away end, that alright?" – "Perfect" and I'm in to see a by now slightly unfamiliar Liverpool team with Ronnie Rosenthal outstanding that day. Coventry take an unlikely early lead, but a hat trick from John Barnes, 2 for Ronnie and of course one for Ian Rush let's me see Liverpool waltz away with a 6-1 away win. I'm guessing the Coventry lads were already on the beach by the second half. A nice enough day all round.

According to my program collection, my second visit was in 1992. This game was memorable for me for only one reason. Seats. I had spent pretty much my entire football watching career to that day watching football stood up. To me sitting down was for old men who couldn't manage to stand any longer. But Coventry loved their seats, and thanks to the Hillsborough report we were all going to have to get used to sitting down – or at least standing in front of a seat and risking shin scabs. The all-seater policy introduced by Jimmy Hill at Coventry in the 70's was later abandoned when Leeds fans (who else) tore-out several hundred seats after losing their First Division game to Coventry City 4–0 in 1981, only months after the seats had been installed. Anyhow. The seats behind the goal were firmly in place in 1992. When we went to our seats we just found a cacophony of arguments about people "sitting in other people's seats". These home fans had had years to get used to it. Was this really the future? I wasn't looking forward to it. I have no idea what happened in the game!

Now its 2001 and I'm back. The third side of the ground for me, but clearly I can never do all 4 now. At least we were all standing! The game was gloriously awful and from about the 60th minute the Bradford fans completely lost interest in the game and decided to sing our way to relegation. For 30 minutes plus stoppage time we sang and we sang and we sang. It was superb. The epitome of being an away fan. This is my team and I am going to sing louder than the home fans, and certainly much longer.

The next day my old friend Patrick Barclay described this match as the "unacceptable face of the premier league". He really isn't a football fan. I have just re read "Bradford City – The Premier League Years" and I am beginning to doubt myself now. They note that Middlesbrough vs Bradford was described as the "unacceptable face of the premier league". Maybe I have misremembered? Maybe the journalists were lazy enough to reuse their tired lines? If I am wrong I of course apologise to Patrick, but that's how I remember it. Poor Middlesbrough – they finished 12th , so a bit harsh on them?

I've not been to Coventry's new ground, the Ricoh – from a distance it looks like the sort of ground I hate.

Leicester

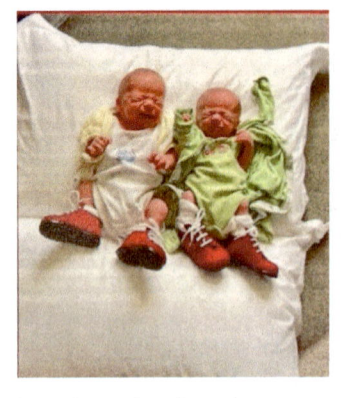

Relegation from the premier league kind of came at a good time for me. After the overspending of BFG in the "6 weeks of madness" coupled with the collapse of ITV digital and the loss of the revenue Bradford would have got for televised second tier games Bradford were heading for a "good ten years of abject misery" as I heard one fan describe it. £35 million in debt and with no likelihood of saviour visible it was always likely to be a long slow drift down the leagues. Hopefully plateauing before non league. I have never managed to fully research this but I think Bradford may be the only team never to have played non league football. When Bradford were formed in 1903 they were admitted straight into the league without ever playing a game. I have never found another team to have done this. So maybe Bradford are the only team never to have played non- league football (so far?)

Anyway, fortunately for me this decline of footballing fortunes in 2002 coincided with the arrival of my twin boys Tom and Sam. This gave me the perfect opportunity to reduce my live football intake at exactly the right time. I did still tick off a few grounds over the next 10 years but they were few and far between.

I never tried to pile on the misery of my own support to my sons, who after all were born in Cheshire. But Pat's mum had an early go by buying them some lovely little Bradford boots for them to wear as babies. Just look at their happy smiling faces as they model them.

I think they could really sense the agonies that awaited them.

I had a mate Eddie (sorry, yet another Eddie), who was a Leicester fan. Well, I say he was a Leicester fan. When I met him I was working in Solihull. Eddie was from somewhere down south, Hatfield? I don't know, somewhere like that and purported to be a Newcastle fan. Then he bought a house in Walsall and became a Walsall fan. In 2002 when we meet up at Leicester, he has relocated with work to the east midlands and so of course is "a bit of a" Leicester fan. He has become one of those people who support "all the local teams". I met up with him again at the Bradford vs Northampton play off final, when of course he was a Northampton fan. I just don't get it. All I can tell you is that all three people I know who have changed the team they support as an adult are all now divorced. No loyalty? You decide.

Bradford were awful and lost 4-0. This did nothing to encourage me to come back anytime soon and I am pleased I missed most of the decade of abject misery. I have 3 boys, they all grew up in this barren spell and for a long time I did nothing to encourage them to follow me to Bradford. Although Pats mum did buy the twins those Bradford shoes when they were babies. For whatever reason, Tom and Eddie have followed me into the pit of despair that is the fate of being a Bradford fan, whilst Sam hedges his bets but really is a Liverpool fan. Who can blame him.

Accrington

I don't know how it came to pass but October 2008 saw me taking Tom and Sam to their first ever Bradford game. And also their first ever away game. Pat said it would be an honour to attend their first ever away game so organised the tickets. I doubt it was that hard. The boys were only a bit past their 6th birthday at the time. God knows what they made of it all.

We stood on a forlorn away terrace with no roof and watched forlorn football (I went back in 2023 and it hasn't changed). We were definitely still in the era of "abject misery" and we lost 2-0. My boys didn't complain of parental cruelty at the end, but neither did they ask to go back. It would take 5 more years for Bradford to wake up. Who would have thought that Sam would see Bradford play twice at Wembley before ever seeing them play at Valley Parade. But again that is another story.

I will just add one thing about the first trip to Wembley for the League Cup final, fourth tier Bradford vs premier league Swansea – unbelievable and of course for non season ticket holders like me, tickets were really hard to come by. Through nefarious means I had managed to secure two tickets and now I had to decide who would go with me. At this stage it was not clear that Tom would become the Bradford fan and Sam wasn't that bothered. So a decision was needed.

I sat them down at the breakfast table. "Here is a piece of paper and a pen each" I said. "Without conferring, write down on your paper the amount of money you would be happy to have, rather than go to the game, then pass your paper to me". They screwed up their 10 year old faces and thought for about a millisecond before scribbling furiously. Sam had written £1 million. Good lad. Tom had written £20. Without a seconds doubt I grabbed my wallet and gave him £20. Crisis averted. This no doubt still rankles with Tom to this day. I owe him a final! Anyway, we all got tickets for the play off final at the end of the same season and we won that one, so that's good isn't it Tom?

Chelsea

A date etched into the memories of all Bradford fans. My Dad was a Chelsea fan and I had always intended Chelsea to be the last of my 92 to round it off with a special day. Well this wasn't the last of the 92 but it certainly turned out to be a special day.

For fans of lower league clubs the FA Cup third round draw is always a big occasion. The chance to dream of that once in a lifetime trips to the Emirates, Etihad or Old Trafford perhaps. As it happens the balls were as unkind as they can be that day and Bradford were drawn away to Millwall. Well that's that for another year, back to thinking about the league...

Without the benefit of my support, Bradford produced a draw at the Den followed by an easy dispatch of the Lions back at our place. Into the hat for Round 4 and out pops Chelsea away – one of those ties we all dream about in the lower leagues.

Unfortunately, without a season ticket I have absolutely no chance of getting in – or so I thought.

Monday evening before the game, Pat calls to say his brother is buying tickets for the Gianfranco Zola suite, £200 a time and do I want to come? Oooh Errr, £200 that's a lot of cash so I ask my wife and she says, "Of course you should go" So that's settled, £200 lighter and I'm off to Stamford Bridge ahead of the 92 schedule – Oh well it looks like Southampton last then, or Sunderland, surely not Luton?

It's a 2 hour train ride down to London for me, so off I go and happen to sit next to a lad and dad off to see Southport play. We get chatting and eventually they ask. "So, do you think you have any chance at all" – "Absolutely not, but I'll be happy if we score a goal" I reply.

Into Euston and a quick 5 minute walk to Kings Cross where I'm meeting Pat. As I'm waiting Martin Keown walks past. Ooh we could do with him defending today I think. Pat arrives and tells me his brother Ed has sorted a pub first before we sample the delights of the £200 buffet. Ed has arranged for us to meet at the White Horse in Parsons Green (known locally as the Sloane Pony so you can tell the normal clientele). We arrive to find Ed looking rather sheepish. "I've just been spot fined £70 for dropping my fag end on the floor and I'm feeling a bit ashamed. Its turning into quite an expensive day". The Sloane Pony is lovely but I'm not sure they enjoyed our visit too much. It's not even 1pm and a Bradford fan is so drunk he can't even stand up, ahh the anticipation.

Time to go to the game – there's a free bar and some food to be eaten. Its less than a 15 minute walk to Stamford bridge through a lovely park so this is all highly recommended. Chelsea is rapidly hitting the heights on my recommendation list, equalled maybe only by Newcastle in the premiership. We hit the Gianfranco Zola suite a little apprehensive as to being surrounded by Chelsea fans, but no such thing. We are surrounded by Scandinavian IT consultants over on a course. "We wanted to see a game and this one was the only one left available – who's playing?" – That's modern football for you.

The game starts to plan, Chelsea race to a two goal lead and we make jolly friends with the few real Chelsea fans sat near us. Then just before half time against the run of play, John Stead swivels and turns delightfully on the edge of the box and places a shot just past Petr Cech. I've got my goal and everyone is happy.

Look at the team sheet that day. Drogba, Salah, Cahill, Azpilicueta. With much much more to come from the bench. And managed by Jose Mourinho. The special one. I was just pleased we had scored.

CHELSEA FC
Official Teamsheet 2014/15

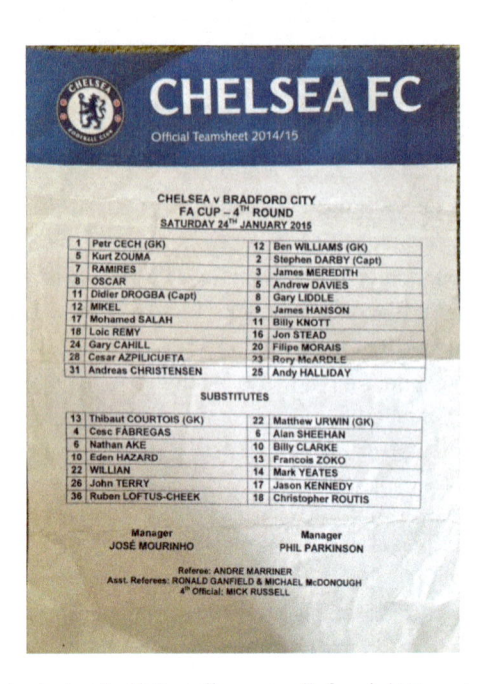

CHELSEA v BRADFORD CITY
FA CUP – 4TH ROUND
SATURDAY 24TH JANUARY 2015

1	Petr CECH (GK)	12	Ben WILLIAMS (GK)
5	Kurt ZOUMA	2	Stephen DARBY (Capt)
7	RAMIRES	3	James MEREDITH
8	OSCAR	5	Andrew DAVIES
11	Didier DROGBA (Capt)	6	Gary LIDDLE
12	MIKEL	9	James HANSON
17	Mohamed SALAH	11	Billy KNOTT
18	Loic REMY	16	Jon STEAD
24	Gary CAHILL	20	Filipe MORAIS
28	Cesar AZPILICUETA	23	Rory McARDLE
31	Andreas CHRISTENSEN	25	Andy HALLIDAY

SUBSTITUTES

13	Thibaut COURTOIS (GK)	22	Matthew URWIN (GK)
4	Cesc FABREGAS	6	Alan SHEEHAN
6	Nathan AKE	10	Billy CLARKE
10	Eden HAZARD	13	Francois ZOKO
22	WILLIAN	14	Mark YEATES
26	John TERRY	17	Jason KENNEDY
36	Ruben LOFTUS-CHEEK	18	Christopher ROUTIS

Manager
JOSÉ MOURINHO

Manager
PHIL PARKINSON

Referee: ANDRE MARRINER
Asst. Referees: RONALD GANFIELD & MICHAEL McDONOUGH
4th Official: MICK RUSSELL

The free alcohol at half time flows, well, freely! We return to our seats a little late and quite a little inebriated. It begins to slowly dawn on us that Bradford are playing really well. Still, Chelsea are a goal to the good and seem quite content to leave us to it. After all, what could possibly go wrong. This continues for a good half hour. Then in the 75th minute, unbelievably Felipe Morais, a Chelsea old boy scores – we are level! – We could get a replay, what a day, What a payday. Ed cheers and there are a few grumbles behind us. Chelsea are now in full panic mode. Mourinho is scowling at his players and they throw everything forward, conjuring a couple of half chances. But throwing everything forward leaves gaps at the back and even more unbelievably, in the 82nd minute Andy Halliday scores. (More of him later). Ed cheers and the grumbles behind turn to a lot of dissatisfied shouting. Pat gets an empty cigarette packet thrown at him – poor Pat, its always him. And it's made clear we better not cheer again. A steward comes and has a quiet word with Ed and he promises to behave.

Chelsea pour forward and both Drogba and Zouma miss great chances and we reach 90 minutes, Surely we will at least get a replay now? The board goes up and its 20 minutes of injury time, 20 minutes! Well, it may have been more like 8 but where did all that come from? As it turns out, no bother, we will just pop up the other end and score a goal worthy of Barcelona at their tik a tak best. 4-2 !. Ed can't control himself and cheers again – sorry Chelsea. To be fair the guys round us were very accommodating but there were some seriously unhappy people behind us, so as soon as the final whistle blows we scurry quickly to the safety of the Gianfranco Zola suite. The front cover shows the Bradford fans away at Chelsea from our expensive and privileged viewpoint.

Ed shouts "Three winners G&Ts please" to a passing waiter who turns out to be an Arsenal fan (Ah, London) and another hour of free alcohol passes in stunned disbelief. We eventually have to tear ourselves away with trains to catch. We wander outside and there is Andy Halliday, the scorer of the winning goal, in just as much of a daze as the rest of us. "Andy" we shout and before he knows it he is being hugged by three middle aged Bradford fans "What just happened" he says. I think he means the game.

At last, back to the train at Euston and I sit in my reserved seat (unusually my actual reserved seat, I usually grab the first one available, just like at a game!) and settle down for a 2 hour journey of happy inebriation. Then, Tony turns up. Tony is a Bradford fan living in the same village as me who I have become vaguely aware of. Tony has of course also been to the game and by a strange coincidence the seat allocations have placed us together. And thus fate takes its course and so begins the Tony years.

The Tony Years

By the Tony years I was no longer buying programmes. So I only have the ones that were handed out for free – well done Colchester. Even Chelsea didn't give me a free programme and my ticket cost £200 !

If you have much better eyesight than me you might just see the Bradford programme on the next page is signed by Ian Ormondroyd. It doesn't really belong in here as it is not an away game but I only have 3 programmes that are less than 15 years old.

By the way, who would have thought that the printed version of the ground breaking 80's Bradford fanzine City Gent would outlast the club matchday programme.

118

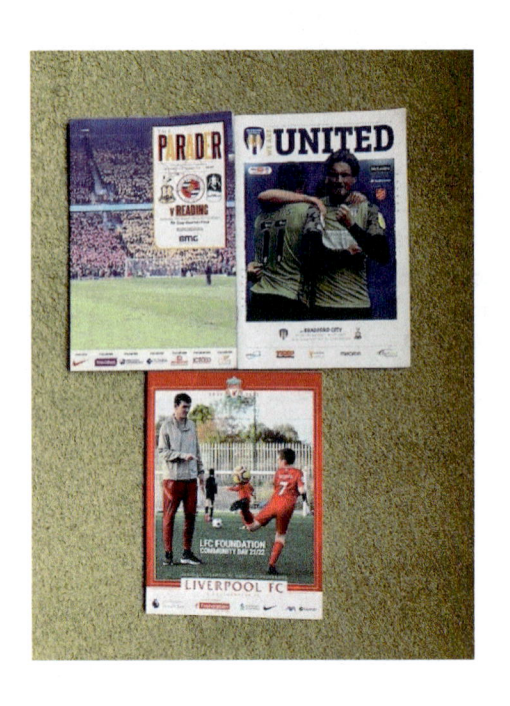

Section Three – The Tony Years, with Tom, Sam and Eddie, 2015 to ?

I first became aware of Tony in December 2014. Theres an annual "Dickensian Event" in my village – very middle class. Held in early December a few hardy locals and lots of complaining junior school children dress up in Victorian clothing and parade through the town. My youngest son, being 8 at the time was a prime candidate for victimisation in this casual cruelty and the rest of us were waiting in the car park for them to get on with it, when up pops Tony. "Ooh I see you have a City scarf on", and so we got chatting for a few minutes and I thought nothing more of it. Then my eldest Tom (well, eldest by 1 minute from his twin brother Sam) comes home to tell me he has been chatting to a City fan outside Sainsburys. "Hello little boy I see you like football" – or some such. I do gather Tony was later castigated thoroughly by his wife. "Are you telling me you went up to and chatted to a 12 year old boy you don't know in the middle of town!" – "Well it seemed perfectly normal to me". That's Tony all over. And then as fate decreed, we bumped into each other again on the train home from Chelsea and it just seemed too hard to fight!

Burton Albion

I started the Tony years with a dismal home game to Chesterfield in 2015, I had forgotten how cold mid week winter games can be and had failed to wrap up properly, but eventually thoughts must always turn to away games. The spreadsheet tells me that the first away game I went to with Tony was Burton Albion. 26th February 2016. This set the pattern for our visits, we share the driving 50/50, but I'm left in sole responsibility of picking the pre match hostelry. In this case the Burton Bridge Inn. A very fine choice indeed and perhaps that is why I was left in charge of the beer. The match itself also followed a familiar pattern over the coming years. Bradford were awful, barely managing to register a decent attempt on goal, but somehow managing to conjure 1 goal and we comfortably lost 3-1. Towards the end the fans amused themselves with a few rounds of "let's pretend we scored a goal in 5, 4, 3 etc" and then going mental – That's the joy of the away end for you.

I did return to Burton in 2022 for an ill-judged visit in the Papa Johns / Johnson Paints / Free Hand Out Trophy (or whatever it's called). This time we lost 4-0, the highlight of the evening was, every time Burton scored, the announcer played "Goal brought to you by Doggie Day Care" causing much amusement and a few rounds of "There's only one Doggie Day Care". The stewards assured us it always goes down a treat. On the way back to my car some Burton fans bellowed "Wanker" at me as they drove past. Presumably because I had a city beanie on rather than through any deep insight into my character. Got to love a football fan. At least it's only an hour home and what else are you going to do on a Tuesday night.

Portsmouth

By now Tony and I are used to each other and he knows all about my long term target to do the 92 with Bradford so I am a soft touch when he says "I've got a friend called Martin, he's a bit of a Portsmouth fan, fancy Portsmouth this weekend". Well, it's about a 4.5 hour drive if you are lucky, so, of course I do! Off we set bright and early in the morning and nice chats and banter were had all the way to the pub and onto the ground.

A word now about food, and Tony. We had two beers and a desultory sandwich in the pub and of course there would be a pie at the ground. Pre Tony I would never eat in the ground as it is always overpriced. However, thanks to Tonys influence I have developed a passion for Pukka pies – especially Chicken Balti. Tony, when we met was still in his full on eating mode so I would have a pie and he would have a pie, a snickers, a cup of tea, and a bag of munchies. Today, Tony declared it to be a two pie day. One for now and one to warm the pocket for later in the game. It's quite often a 2 pie day, especially if we are losing.

Portsmouth started the game well and slowly began to dominate, but the ball wouldn't go into the net for them. Around the 80th minute I've given up hope and turn to Tony – "We wouldn't score if we played until next Tuesday". Sure enough within 4 seconds we pop up the other end and score a goal – its total robbery and we all know it. At least Martin is in with the home fans so we don't have to apologise. What a quiet drive home we had. I think Martin managed to say he thought we were a bit lucky, by the time we reached Oxford.

Millwall – The Old and the New

On the 11th April 1989 I went into the Lion's den for the first time. With fresh faced youthful vigour – just another game at another ground – right? Millwall versus Liverpool. This was the Sheringham and Cascarino Millwall team versus the Barnes, Beardsley and Aldridge Liverpool. So this was lined up to be a cracking match, no doubt. I was in London visiting my mate Stevie– an Arsenal fan with a stutter. (Important point) and as usual I wanted to visit a new ground. To Stevie's horror and my delight the only game available on this Tuesday night was Millwall versus Liverpool. With Stevie muttering darkly about trouble we headed off and arrived at the tube station to be met by an entire cavalry unit of mounted police and an infantry division of foot soldiers of indeterminate loyalty. We headed off to the away end and a policeman barked at us – "What team are you" in a strong London accent so I didn't get the question immediately. "Err err errr" stuttered Stevie. Who I should also note was doing a great impression of looking like a hooligan at this point. He was working as a cycle courier around London and had recently fallen off his bike and lost both his font teeth and his face looked a treat!, "err err err" he continued to stutter – Then eventually to his delight he came up with an answer – "ah ah arsenal!" – This was not the answer the police were looking for but by now I had caught up. "Liverpool" – I said, "it's ok – he's with me" – We were treated to some very suspicious looks but allowed to go into the ground.

Although Millwall took an early lead Liverpool recovered and won the game 2-1, the home support being not best pleased about all this. With my youthful exuberance we headed for the exit, which was firmly locked. Twenty minutes later we were still heading nowhere. "You really don't want to be going out there" was all we got from the stewards. Eventually we were allowed out nearly an hour after the game once the mounted cavalry had dispersed the enthusiastic locals. Well at least that was off the list – I wouldn't be back would I?

Fast forward 27 years to the 20th May 2016, Bradford have wobbled unconvincingly into the Division 1 play offs but managed to lose the first leg at home 3-1 due to a barmy 10 minute spell. "We have to go to Millwall – you never know" says my mate Tony. He's got a fair point. In 1996 we lost the home leg of the play offs 2-0 to Blackpool only to win the return 3-0 and it was the same pattern when we beat Burton. So off we go.

In my defence I was on a potent cocktail of drugs at the time awaiting a back operation, Gabapentin, Tramadol and Amitriptyline – essentially, I was completely stoned on opiates and I am sure I made for a very interesting travel companion. You can see me and Tony below. Right in the middle. Do I look stoned?

Off we drove to London Bridge and a pleasant pint or two in the Shipwrights arms. Then it was time for the game, onto the tube line – so far so good, then on to the tube train. A low guttural moan was started up and suddenly half the train were chanting: "Mooooonnnnnnnnnnk". This is nice, said my opiates to no one in particular and Tony tried his best to look inconspicuous. Into the ground via an iron bar covered walkway with Millwall fans chanting pleasantries and throwing God knows what in our direction and we are up on the top tier (thankfully).

The game ends 1-1, cue the Millwall tribe on to the pitch to come and taunt us. I think through my opiate haze that they just wanted to make friends. "Aren't they lovely" I said and off we went for a 4 hour drive home – That's football, but at least surely I won't be back? – Please don't move ground again.

Wimbledon. In three parts

Wimbledon have the dubious honour of being the away team I have seen play home games at the most number of stadia. It is rarely a good thing to have moved grounds more than once. I have seen Bradford have to play home games at the Bradford rugby league ground (Odsal) as well as at Leeds and Huddersfield after the fire. And I have seen Wimbledon play at Crystal Palace and at Kingston before finally making it back to Plough Lane.

Perhaps the first game wasn't even AFC Wimbledon (as they now are), but in my mind they are. For me it's the fans that define the team, everything else changes. But the fans stay. No matter that you have sold "the franchise". In Wimbledon part 1 at Crystal Palace, we lose 3-2. It had been a miserable drive down. Setting off early to allow pub time, the M6 was closed and I only just got there for kick off. 7 hour drive – great. In the game we were totally outplayed and losing 3-1 with the match coming to a close. Up pops Dean Windass with a last minute consolation and we decide to head to the pub as the final whistle goes. After all I've missed my pre-match drink. As usual the pub is full of

Bradford fans. We like our beer! Amongst the chat we notice that the BBC is way behind on the scores. The game is shown as 3-1 and still playing[3]. Then at about 5-20 – half an hour late. Dean Windass is shown as scoring, 3-2. The pub bursts into song, "We're gonna score in a minute". Football humour. Pat's brother Eddie is really drunk for once and insists on singing John Hartson is a tw£t to the tune of Ilkley Moor Bah Tat. More football humour.

Wimbledon part two was at the wonderfully named Cherry Red Records Fans stadium. And a proper roller coaster ride it was. The pre match entertainment (obviously) was a massive womble wandering free around the stadium, "what the f is that" sang our younger fans, Gosh I'm old. But it didn't take the game long to set alight. We were ahead in 3 minutes and level 10 minutes later. The game then settled down. It became a little steady and maybe the ref was bored? He awarded a penalty to Wimbledon in 68th minute – 2-1 to them. On rushes an unwise Wimbledon fan pitch invader. Arrested and carted off. The ref awards a penalty to us and we equalise. Then in the 90th minute big James Hanson pops up to score a last minute winner. Happy days. I wonder when the pitch invader found out they had lost? If you look carefully at the footage for the winning goal on the EFL show or YouTube you can see me jumping up and down in the away "side", but definitely not on the pitch.

Offside Ref – We used to laugh at people who didn't understand the offside rule. Now I don't think anyone understands it. Midway through the second half, before scoring his winner, James Hanson was given offside in his own half. Not being one to let the facts get in the way of a good shout I started giving the ref a good old earful. The guy behind me trying to patiently

---

[3] Apparently the delay was because they weren't sure if the ref had blown the final whistle before Windass had scored.

explain that you are offside if you run back into your own half from an offside position and then attempt to play the ball. Really, is that what offside is about. Surely it was designed to stop goal hangers? Now you have to worry if your armpit hair is too long, whether you have interfered with play, whether the defenders touch was a deliberate attempt to play the ball backwards or was a deflection off of an attackers pass. Whether you are in a passive position and whether you are interfering with the goalies sight line. As big Ron used to say. If you are not interfering with play what are you doing on the pitch. Let's just go back to the old rules. Anyway, it made no difference to the outcome of the game…

I suppose after seeing 2-3 and 3-2, it may have been inevitable. Plough Lane was a bit of a let down for me. When the train from Warrington is running well it's a smooth 1 hour 45 minutes to Euston, but it doesn't run well all that often. We arrive at Warrington to find our train is cancelled. No real surprise. Right, short train journey to Crewe and catch a London train from there. At 5 to 11 the departures board is showing the train leaves at 11. At 1 minute to 11 the train just disappears from the screen. Just disappears. How can that be? Oh, they couldn't find a driver a helpful guard tells us? Hmmm. We are now over an hour late. Fortunately, I'm on dry January so I am not missing valuable drinking time. We eventually get to Euston well over an hour late. At least that means I get a full refund on our train tickets so it's a cheap day out. It's a mere 14 stops on the northern line to get near to the new Wimbledon ground. 14 stops on the northern line is reason enough for me never to work in London. It's hot, overcrowded, dilapidated, and everybody looks so miserable! We do eventually get to the ground and its nice enough.

I don't know if it's just me but have they tried to make the front look like Wimbledon tennis courts? The game itself is a dreary 0-

0. Bradford have a guy sent off but this does nothing to raise Wimbledon out of their lethargy and everyone seems happy with a point. I suppose after 10 goals in the first two games that's only fair.

On the way out it becomes clear (to me) that the police are new to this and don't quite have their routine sorted. Wimbledon versus Bradford is not a high risk game for trouble but this is the biggest crowd they have ever seen at this ground and they are nervous. They have blocked the way to the home end which unfortunately is also the way to the tube station. They then send us up a dead end (deliberately?). Eventually we make a torturous circle around the police line and re-mingle with the Wimbledon fans. There is no trouble, everyone is happy. Thanks police – please sort this for next time. I tell this story to a friend who is a Wimbledon fan and he says, "Police or stewards" – "Police why?" – Oh we had to sack our last stewards as they were too rough with away fans and broke someone's arm. Lovely. I can't actually find proof of this, so maybe it didn't happen? The stewards were great with us – as they almost always are.

I would however add to this a report from a Walsall fan for their game at Wimbledon at the end of the 23/24 season –
"*Footballing performances aside, today has to go down as one of the worst match day experiences that I have ever been to in all of my years watching us play. The operation, actions and attitude of the stewarding and security staff towards our fans was absolutely appalling. They might as well have called themselves the bloody Gestapo. In the first instance, their stop and search outside of the ground was more thorough, forensic and intrusive than any police*

check or airport security check that anyone will ever have. They even made me get my wallet out and started combing through that, which during this process, made plenty of Walsall fans late getting into the ground. Secondly, after entering through the turnstile and making it inside the stadium, they then had 7/8 stewards dictating to and making everyone pull out and show their tickets just to get from the concourse to pitch side! Absolutely ridiculous level of power mongering. I know of fans that went to the toilet before the game from their seats and stewards wouldn't let them back to pitch side again because their partner had their tickets. It felt like at every moment inside the ground and during the game, their stewards and security staff were doing anything they could to impose, intimidate, alienate and aggravate our fans. I struggled to concentrate on the game with all of their pacing and patrolling back and forth and scowling looks at us. I genuinely felt like we were all a group of caged and contained animals in that stand. The frustrating thing is that the large majority of our fans were absolutely no bother to anyone and caused no issues, hassle or harm and posed no threat to anyone. There was no tension, atmosphere or needle that warranted this treatment at all. The irony was that their fans were launching and throwing stuff onto the pitch before Hutch's penalty with no recourse! Then to top it all off, upon exiting, they then proceeded to send all Walsall fans on a 15/20 minute detour out of the ground. Once I protested, they made no exception for the fact that I was on crutches at the game after having knee surgery. Treated with complete disdain and contempt from start to finish. I can categorically say that I will never be re-visiting that ground ever again."

Oh dear. I shall not be rushing back.

Macclesfield

Sadly Macclesfield are now a long way from league football. It's just a short drive from my house (20 miles) and has some great pubs. We set off to the game on a very crisp cold November Saturday (30/11/19) to what turns out to be Macclesfield's last (ever?) game against Bradford. We never played them at home that season (who was guessing COVID would happen). But quite a few fans were muttering darkly about what was happening to Macclesfield. I had done my research and found us a truly lovely pub across the park from the ground. Tony instantly fell in love with the stout. I had driven us proudly to the game in my new company car, a 100% electric E-Golf. This turned out to be either a big mistake or a stroke of genius depending on your perspective.

We parked up in a back street by the pub and as we were leaving the car I looked back and decided to repark the car. I never do this. I have never done it before or since. I went back to the car and it would not start. It was dead. It was deader than the Monty Python parrot. It was clearly going nowhere. On the other hand we were clearly going to the pub and the game. It was 1.30 so I rang the AA, who with their usual swiftness said they would have a man there about 4. So we had a couple of pints, went to watch the game and I left at half time with Bradford losing 1-0. On the bright side the AA guy turned up bang on 4 pm. Took one look at the car and said. "I won't be able to fix this – I don't know why they send me out to these (Electric Vehicles). You will have to be towed home". Ok. Plan B. It's too late to go back to the game, so it's into the pub. On the plus side, the beer is great, the pub does food and the AA will drive us home. I haven't yet mentioned that my 13 year old son Eddie was with us. He was having the time of his life. Watching his dad and his mate drink 6 or 7 beers in a lovely pub with all the chips and pizza he could eat. Eventually the AA tow truck turns up about 9 pm. "I can't get the tow truck down there – we are going to have to push" says the new AA guy. It is now snowing. So me, Tony and the AA guy are heaving a 2 tonne car while Eddie sits in the driving seat steering. "Best. Day. Ever." Says Eddie. We finally get back home about 9-30 and we pretty much have to pour Tony out of the tow truck cab. He wobbles off home happy. Two footnotes. Bradford drew the game – I seem to make a habit of missing goals – maybe I should stop watching? The car took two weeks to fix. I haven't had an electric vehicle since. But I have had a Hydrogen car. But that's an earlier story.

Rochdale

Rochdale is less than 7 miles from Oldham. In many ways they are similar north Manchester towns. Indeed they are on very similar trajectories football wise and probably economically too, both unfortunately in the national league at time of writing. Yet for all the world they are different places to me. I have never enjoyed a trip to Oldham's boundary park and I have never failed to enjoy a trip to Rochdale's Spotland. My favourite trip was for an essentially pointless game at the end of the season. In 2017 Bradford had already qualified for the play offs with a game to spare. However, other teams, including Rochdale, still had something to play for. So Sky (I assume) had decreed that this last set of third tier games would all kick off at 12 noon on a Sunday. This is not a promising kick off time for somebody who likes a couple of pints before the game. In the week running up to the game I rang my favourite Rochdale pub (I shall not name it) and asked if they would be open (yes from 10-30 they confirmed). So Tony and I turn up just before 11 on the Sunday morning and the door is locked. Peering through the window I can just about work out that in fact there are people drinking inside. So we wander round the back and get in through the kitchens. Two pints please! They obviously couldn't get (or couldn't be bothered to get) an early license but opened just the same. Perfect.

Judging from the atmosphere in the away end, none of the Bradford fans had had any problem finding liquid refreshment that day. It was electric, nothing to worry about and the fans were in the mood for fun. "We're going up and the Leeds are staying down" we all sang. Ah well, there is only hope after all. As the game was meaningless we had chosen to rest 10 of our normal starting 11. I have never been a fan of resting players, especially when the game is a week away. They need to be sharp and used to playing with each other in my view. Ironically on this day, a week before Bradford played Fleetwood in the play off semi-final first leg 21 players who started in that game were rested. The one exception was Rory McCardle. And guess who scored the only goal in the Bradford Fleetwood first leg – yes that's right – Rory! And so, we leave Rochdale behind for now, for the promised land of the league 1 play offs. But I really hope to be back some day.

Fleetwood

What makes a good away day? For me, it's got to have the following ingredients:

- Good transport links – I don't mind travelling a long way if I have to but I hate sitting in a traffic jam for an hour when I'm close to the ground or in a vast queue of humanity waiting for my chance to get on a tube for the best part of 2 hours. This takes a lot of premiership grounds off my list.
- At least one great pub choice – I am happy to walk quite a long way. Or even in extreme circumstances, Park up, drink and then drive a bit closer.
- A good atmosphere – Not brutally unwelcoming where you feel in fear for your life, but definitely with a bit of a vibe.
- A nice pie

Clearly some of these things evolve over time from club to club. Some grounds are harshly demolished as the club moves to a soulless out of town stadia. Pubs come and go. I love this place or I hate that place can change. But. I love Fleetwood. It is easy to get to, easy to get away from afterwards and it has the most awesome pub. The Strawberry Gardens. Syd Little (Yes him) no longer does the food there but he helped in the renaissance of this pub and it is excellent. And you can get parked near here, have a couple of excellent pints, walk to the game. And get home again in very little time. What is not to like?

So needless to say I have been a few times. It's an intimate ground, which is great for a bit of banter. One night we were playing there and the Fleetwood keeper at the time was called Maxwell. "You're just a shit cup of coffee" we all sang. For a bit of a laugh, as the game was poor. You have four options as a sportsman when the crowd has a go at you. Ignore it, Use it to motivate you, get annoyed, or in my opinion, the best option, have a laugh back. We had a great natter with Chris Maxwell that night. He is now in the Championship so good luck to him.

Our best time at Fleetwood was the play off semis. Although we nearly didn't get to go. Fleetwood is a small ground and so the away ticket allocations were not huge. At the time the Bradford scheme was to have "Priority members" – You paid a fee and allegedly got priority for games that would sell out. Tony and I had priority membership and had got tickets for the league game no bother.

But when it came to the allocation for the play off semi the tickets seemed to mysteriously vanish. Certainly Tony and I weren't getting in the away end. Annoyingly, Fleetwood were struggling to sell out their home end and indeed in the end didn't get close to selling out.

The club did sensibly realise that they could be overrun by Bradford fans in the wrong end so brought in a condition that you could only buy home tickets with proof of a local postcode. We all trawled through our address books to find a mate with a local postcode and I found one (who I hadn't seen for 30 years mind) but then, even better was to come. Tony works as a physio and he was training a "lad" who happened to be a footballer at Fleetwood coming to the end of his career. "No bother lads I will get you some comps". So the matchday finds us at the Strawberry Gardens clutching our "Wives and Girlfriends" tickets which you can see in this beautifully cropped photo of Tony! The Strawberry Gardens is predictably rammed with Bradford fans – we like our real ale in Bradford. I got talking to a few of the fans and of course was interested to know how they had got tickets and a common theme emerged – "Through Bingley Bantams" – "Through Shipley Bantams" etc, I later accused the club of this on a Facebook post and it was vigorously denied – all I know is I didn't get a ticket. The club has since moved to a loyalty points system and so far this seems to work for me. It does still attract a lot of moaning, mostly from people who never go to away games!

On the day, Tony is massively over excited and I love him for it. At one point he goes off to buy his round and comes back with 4 pints. There are only 2 of us. "They just gave me them Duncs – I couldn't say no, I'm driving so you better drink them!". Suitably lubricated we set off to the game itself. I have sat in a WAGs section once before – at Glasgow Rangers. It is a weird experience as, no matter what the game, most WAGS have no interest in what is happening. There was one lady who was desperately excited and we tried to remain friendly. The rest were more interested in their nails and smartphones. Bradford were 1-0 up from the first leg and fortunately the game passed with very little incident. The game ended a very satisfying 0-0 and the Fleetwood fans filtered out disappointedly. We made our way along the emptying ground towards the away end to find that there were about 200 Bradford fans in our stand who had quietly or in some cases less quietly done the same as us. What a day. In some respects the last great day that we have had as Bradford fans.

Yeovil

Oh why, oh why, oh why did we decide to go to Yeovil? At the time we had made the play offs twice in a row and Yeovil were on a downward trajectory. Add to that this looked like an easy win (on paper) and a chance to make the 4th round FA cup draw and a glamour tie. So we couldn't say no. Little did we know that the wheels, which in truth had been getting looser and looser since May, were finally going to completely come off the Bradford bus.

Its over 4 hours to Yeovil, we set off nice and early and stopped at the delightful Gloucester services. If you haven't been you should go. This is how all motorway services should be. Tony loved it, so a good omen. I do like a good omen on an away trip. We got to the pub in plenty of time, a chain pub, Harvester or some such. Filled with Bradford fans who had booked lunch in advance. So it's not just me that plans in advance. The talk in the pub was excited optimism. Yeovil were in terrible form and had an injury crisis which meant they didn't even have a full team. This being January they had drafted in some emergency replacements. But they hadn't even met each other. This was surely going to be a walkover. We left the pub for the fish and chip shop and made our way happily along to the ground. That's where we heard the creaking noises as the wheels fell off.

Enough has been written about Edin Rahic and I don't want to get sued, so look it up elsewhere. Suffice to say that at this point it became clear that Rahic would no longer back McCall at all. In retrospect, McCall had worked miracles this season to keep us challenging for the play offs with a weak squad. But now we were in the transfer window, McCall wanted to do some badly needed business. The first thing was to get Luke Hendrie resigned for the remainder of the season. This would have cost buttons. But it wasn't sanctioned.

It was a cold day as you can see. It didn't warm us when we heard the team news that there was no Hendrie. From our perspective as fans this was where the players simply gave up. We fell off the cliff in spectacular style. We lost 2-0 that day to a lower league team who didn't even know each other. We lost the next few games and McCall got sacked. "Maybe I deserve the sack for the recent results, but I deserve a medal for what I achieved before that" he mused. From 5th in January we drifted to 11th by the end of the season. The next season we finished plum bottom and were relegated. How to ruin a club.

So a 4 hour drive back home. Not in the best of spirits we turned on Talk Sport to listen to the "wisdom" of Robbie Savage. There were two hot stories that day that dominated the phone in. Liverpool were about to sell Coutinho for £150 million or so and the scousers were all up in arms about how this was a disaster. Well, how wrong can you be, the money allowed them to build a title winning team. The second story was Mark Hughes. Mark was managing premier league Stoke, but the fans were not happy! Stoke had just been dumped out of the FA Cup (Ha, join the club) by lower league Coventry and the fans had had enough. For 3 hours as we drove home we had Stokie after

Stokie calling in to demand Hughes was sacked. After 3 hours we had had enough and so had Savage. Right that's it he said (as a bit of a mate of Mark), no more discussion of Mark tonight. Ten minutes later he was proved to have been premature. "I know we said we wouldn't mention Mark Hughes again tonight, but I have to tell you that we have just heard he has been sacked" Cue more Stokies ringing in. Little did we know or have any way of guessing that in less than 5 years Hughes would be our manager and after a year or so it would be us calling for him to go.

Of course, Yeovil Town drew Man Utd away in the next round of the FA Cup. Of course they did. What a jackpot.

Gillingham

No disrespect to Gillingham, but it's just not a place that you would think to visit twice. If you live in the North. It's not in London, it's the wrong side of London. Every year now I look at who's coming up from the National League and just hope it's not Dover or any other team on the wrong side of London. Sorry Dover! Unsurprisingly then, I have been to Gillingham twice. The first trip was in October 2018. Bradford are woeful and are in freefall after the wild excesses of our erstwhile Pep Guardiola. The man himself, Edin "I know football" Rahic. Well, he certainly knew how to get us relegated and this game helped us nicely on the way. We lost the game 5-0 and in truth we were lucky to get 0. "You're just a shit Andy Carroll" we sang at their 6 foot 3 centre forward Tom Eaves for a bit. Til he demolished us. 38 goals in 84 games for the Gills. We should be so lucky.

You can't mention Gillingham without a note on their "away end". As you can see, it is built of temporary scaffolding (Can you get permanent scaffolding?) and is uncovered. I wonder if this is what Lord Justice Taylor had in his mind when he forced all seater stadia on us – whether we wanted it or not. There is usually a redeeming feature about an away game and this one was undoubtedly the travel. 10 minute walk to the station. 30 minutes into St Pancras. 5 minutes run from St Pancras to Euston virtually NFL style mashing people out of the way. 1 hour 50

Euston to Warrington, and back home in front of the telly before 8-30. It would probably take me longer to get home from Man City – and its only 15 miles away.

Gillingham mk2 was a very different affair. I was "working in London" which these days means working from home and trying to minimise trips to the office. "Oh, you should come to the office" – Why? - so I can sit in a cubicle and talk to people over the internet? Bizarre. Anyway, my work bosses were getting increasingly angsty about me spending more time in London so I spotted an opportunity. Gillingham away on a Tuesday night and kip over at my mate Adam's house. February 23 and it's a cold dark drizzly evening. My Good beer guide has left me short. The pub it recommends closes at 7 pm on a Tuesday night (what kind of place is this?). So I resort to the official away fans guide on the Bradford City website. This is a big mistake. I've done this twice now and it hasn't ended well either time. Bradford are recommending 2 pubs. The first is near the station. So off we trot. Well this is a strange pub, it has no doors! It turns out the landlord has got concerned about the number of fans wanting a beer and decided his pub is full. All doors locked. The second pub is up near the ground. So off we trot again. In the drizzle. Getting a bit wet and cold now and mindful that we are going to be sat on open scaffolding for 2 hours. We arrive at the second pub. It clearly hasn't been open since COVID struck – great lads, thanks. By now there is no option but into the ground and 2 bottles of Heineken. Fortunately this is where the night improves. The Gills have taken pity on us. The scaffolding is closed and we are all housed under a lovely roof at the side of the ground. Even better, they gift us an early goal and then we score another. We can dream of promotion. Gillingham, I wonder if I will be back?

Newport

Newport away. I should have done this in the 90's. A quick drive along the M4 from Swindon and the box would be ticked. But in 2020 Bradford hadn't played Newport since 1985 since Newport were languishing in various non league environments, in fact not even playing in Wales for several years. After fighting their way back to league status in February 2020, I finally got the chance. It was time to plan. 3 hour drive each way, if you get lucky with traffic, or train. Train it is then. Change at Crewe and get on one of British Rails finest. I say British Rail because I am absolutely certain that this train is old enough to have been old when British Rail was still going. Two hours on a rickety 3 carriage train with 1 toilet if you're lucky. Well, at least it's not busy. Or at least it wasn't busy until Shrewsbury. There is some Rugby Union thingy going on at Cardiff and the entire English fan base seems to be based in Shrewsbury. The train is absolutely rammed but this doesn't stop the bunch sat opposite us. Out comes the Fortnum and Mason hamper, champagne, blinis, foie gras, it's certainly not a Pukka Pie for them! I start up some rugby vs football banter with them and Eddie cringes with embarrassment, but they take it in good jest. By the time we get near Newport the train is so jammed you can barely get up from the seat. We start early and it takes us a good 5 minutes to get to the doors. "Why would you want to get off in Newport" comes the chorus from the rest of the carriage. Why indeed. But I have a plan.

Newport is home to the Tiny Rebel brewery, one of my favourite craft beer brewers. And they have a brewery tap. You really must try it. I recommend "Pump Up the Jam". The food is also excellent.

Stuart McCall is our manager (again). He regularly comes back in our hour of need and he has inherited a pretty poor squad. Not that it will matter as the season will be cancelled for COVID soon. I wonder if he will be back for another managerial stint? I think John Sheridan holds the record for most managerial spells, at Oldham?

The reason I mention this is for the idiocy that we are about to witness. The game is drifting aimlessly as many games at this level tend to do and we suddenly become aware of activity in the dug outs over on the other side of the pitch. Stuart is pointing and shouting angrily at the crowd. Unbelievably there is a man in the main stand with the Newport fans, holding a big Leeds United flag and hurling abuse at Stuart. Stuart is a seasoned manager and is therefore used to getting a fair bit of grief from home fans and you would normally expect him to just ignore it, but he is incensed. Obviously we couldn't hear what was said, but it was apparently abuse about the Bradford fire. McCall was not going to take that. There were plenty of Newport stewards around and they did nothing. Newport eventually apologised. Newport, not impressed, Leeds not surprised. That guy with the Leeds flag must have been waiting since 1985 for that moment? There really is no understanding some people.

Walsall

It has taken me a while but I have come to love Walsall away. My first trip to the Bescot was a Tuesday night in the 90's, very unappealing and these sentiments were reconfirmed when Pat and I visited in 2003. A soulless out of town stadium stuck in an industrial estate although it is handily close to the M6. Twenty years on from these unpromising visits and Tony is pestering to go, it's a Tuesday night again and what else are we going to do? Walsall is only an hour away so we should give it a go. There must be a good option for a pub if we make some extra effort? That's when I discover the Black Country Arms. Heaven. Twenty cask ales on hand pump. It's in the town centre, so a bit of a pain as the ground is about 2 miles away. But if you get a Tuesday night game you can park right outside the pub then drive the mile and a half or so to near the ground and still get close enough even 10 minutes before kick-off. That's the joys of a crowd base of 4,000. On a Saturday, park at the Asda – its £1.

It was so good I went back. This time under cover of a work trip to the NEC and then a train ride to Walsall where I'd arranged to meet Tony who would drive down with my son Eddie. This worked a treat, only I'd already had 2 pints when Tony arrived and 4 pints is a lot for me these days. It probably didn't help with the language barriers!

Tony downed a swift couple and we scooted off up to the ground, perilously close to kick off and still needing a pie. The pie queue was about 10 deep, but we would just make it. I peered down at the kiosk and could see the pie racks were empty, disaster! It looked like they only had hot dogs left. We got to the front eventually and asked for 3 hot dogs. "Sorry love, only 1 left". Oh no. So we gave that to Eddie, being gentlemen. What were Tony and I going to eat? "What have you get left that's hot?" I asked. "Poys" came the reply. "I'm sorry, what are poys?" I'm afraid I said. She took it well. "Steak poys, meat and potato poys or cheese poys, you know". "Ah, pies!" I insisted on saying, but we still got served.

And so, on to the game. I know I have moaned about this before, and Bradford are worse than most at this, but..

I simply do not understand why fans insist on trying to get on the backs of former players, especially strikers, and especially the ones with "attitude". We know how this script ends. Sure enough, its 1-1 heading towards 90 minutes. Andy Cook, our striker (ex-Walsall) has been getting grief all game. He pops into the box, gets knocked down, gets a penalty, puts it away. 2-1 win. He milks the home fans for all they are worth. We really should all learn and just shut up when ex-players visit.

The next time we visited, Sam came over from Birmingham to meet us at the pub. Eddie and I were already enjoying a pint and one of their excellent sandwiches when Sam showed up. I sent him to the bar with my credit card and instructions to get a sandwich. He came back predictably with the most expensive beer on offer, but also with a complaint. The language barrier had stuck again. "I asked for a sandwich but they said they didn't have any – they only have a "Batch?" – it looks like a sandwich to me – or a barm or a bun, oh well. Anyway, I really like Walsall. And the fact I can get home in an hour is a bonus.

Doncaster

The first time I visited Doncaster was 2005. This was their old ground. A nice enough place but not one I have particularly clear memories of. Probably because Bradford were on a dismal slide towards what looked like it could eventually become oblivion. The one abiding memory was the music. Tony Christie is a local lad in Doncaster and although this was before the days when Peter Kaye et al really repopularised the song, they ran on to the pitch to "Is this the way to Amarillo". The crowd joined in with some gusto. Cracking song to get us all going. Bradford should try something similar, but what would we use? Kiki Dee "Don't go breaking my heart" – perhaps not.

Plans were already in place to move when the ground was half demolished in a gas explosion in 2007. Now it is a housing estate and all traces of the original ground are gone. Sad. They say you can sometimes still hear Tony Christie at 7.44 on a Tuesday night..

I wouldn't be back in Doncaster until February 2023. Doncaster is now another modern out of town stadium, but this time one I have some affection for. It does help to love a ground when you win. The day hadn't started particularly auspiciously. I'd decided we should travel by train so I booked us three cheap tickets on Northern trains, for me, Tony and Eddie, we would pass through Sheffield where we would meet up with Tom (now at Uni there) Toms mate Archie (Brentford fan) and Pat. Best laid plans. We get to the station to find that the Northern Line train going has been cancelled, but there is a Trans Pennine Express train, so we hop on that. Big no no apparently. The officious ticket inspector makes me buy three more tickets to Sheffield where we will change and maybe catch a Northern train. You have got to love our train system? We get to Sheffield a fair few quid down and meet up with Tom and his mate. As soon as we get on this train the ticket inspector grabs us so I proceed to regale him with the story so far. He is totally sympathetic and we spend the entire journey bemoaning the actions of the first ticket inspector. His parting shot as we leave the train in Doncaster is that he suggests I should have not paid and demanded to meet the transport police. This seemed like a high risk strategy to me but we find ourselves at Doncaster station with a few minutes to kill as we wait for Pat to turn up on his train. So I find some police to ask what they would have done. "No idea mate - we aren't transport police". So we will never know.

The policing that day was "high presence". There was a rail offer that meant Bradford fans could get to Doncaster for a fiver. Consequently the away end, which is well over 3,000, would be sold out. There would be nearly as many Bradford as Doncaster fans. So it should be a cracking atmosphere we thought, and it certainly was.

Off we go to a nice enough pub around the corner from the station for a pint. We drink one, but decide we can do better. So we wander off and find the Queen Crafthouse. A lovely pub that I heartily recommend if you are passing. Toms mate is a Brentford fan and rapidly getting used to premiership games. He is agog that away fans can just wander around town and go in any pub they chose. Sounds like I might not enjoy the prem any more?

Finally, onto the game, It's a bit over a mile to walk to the ground. The worst bit being that all pedestrians are funnelled down one tiny alleyway at one point. Who designs these travel plans for modern stadia? Are we supposed to arrive by helicopter? The game does not disappoint. The away end is full. So everyone stands and the atmosphere is raucous. Even better we win, and the train journey home is uneventful.

Morecambe

For many Bradfordians, Morecambe occupies a special place in their hearts. It used to be called "Bradford by the sea". With a direct train link from Bradford it was the easiest seaside trip available. You used to be able to get the local Bradford newspaper (The T&A) in most Morecambe newsagents and for the "Wakes week" in Bradford when the mills were closed for a week's shut down there would be more Bradfordians in

Morecambe than in Bradford. Morecambe has largely suffered like all northern seaside towns with the rise of cheap foreign holidays and it is now mostly a town of "former glories".

The Good Beer Guide gives little optimism for a good away day anywhere near the ground so again I follow the Bradford City Website suggestion. This is again a big mistake. The pub is absolutely rammed with Bradford fans. If you did manage to get to the bar you would be rewarded with a pint of nasty lager in a plastic cup. This is not the place for me, so we beat a hasty retreat and go off to explore. We find The Exchange pub. Not particularly inviting from the outside but heaven on the inside. Five cask ales on hand pump, a place to sit and the early game live on Sky. This is what I am looking for!

I've been to Morecambe twice now. The first was better. Before the game, as the teams run out, there is always some music. Every club has an option. Pick something traditional? Local? Uplifting? Awful. For some reason Notts Forest play Mull of Kintyre – a dreadful choice in my opinion. Not really up to 7 nation army is it? In the Rahic era we had some Wagnerian opera briefly, Anyway. The first time I went to Morecambe they played The Morecambe and Wise theme tune. All the over 40's in the crowd happily singing "Bring Me Sunshine" at the top of their voices whilst the youth look on in disbelief and wonder what the f is going on. Last time round they didn't play it. It ruined my day!

Stevenage and Cheltenham

By now I am up to 80 grounds of the current 92. The remainder, apart from Bolton, fall into two categories. They are either a very long way, or they are both a long way away and are also teams that I assume, if I wait long enough, they will fall out of the league and I won't have to visit them. Of course, eventually you just have to bite the bullet and do the miles. Away at Stevenage on a Tuesday night in February isn't a difficult game to get tickets to. A little creative diary management and I have manoeuvred some work around so I happen to need to spend an overnight north of London on the 8th February – so the game is on. I don't know who designed Stevenage new town but they certainly did not do it with the pedestrian in mind. I am stopping within a mile of the ground just off the A1, but it's impossible to walk to the ground as it's all dual carriageway and the usual array of Dunelm Mills and Argos outlets. No matter, Stevenage has an excellent free car park right by the ground so I park up and walk into town. Again, there really aren't good options, its either the dual carriageway or a dark and dingy underpass for the mile into town. Nothing's going to deter me from a pre match pint so it's into the underpass and off to the quite excellent Chequers for enough beer to see me through the coming rigours.

The abolition of re-election in 1986 had been a mixed blessing. But it has certainly added to the grounds I get to visit. Some, like Stevenage have grown relatively organically and they rise and fall with the natural tide. It is the other sort I dislike, the teams driven by a wealthy owner with little or no community involvement. Eventually the owner will die or lose interest and the place disappears. Maybe I should admit they all deserve a chance?

You can never say never in football because you don't know what play offs may have in store for you, but on the whole Stevenage is in that category of "I've been and I doubt very much whether I will be going back".

Cheltenham in some ways is a much better bet. It has a lot of good pubs on offer. But it's just such a long way, and for me the wrong side of the M5/M6 junction which means your journey time could be anything. To tick Cheltenham off my list I found myself a Tuesday night game, manoeuvred a relatively sensible work conference meeting at the NEC into my diary and got myself to Cheltenham in fine order. I sat in quiet contemplation for the game as we watched our team fight valiantly and lose 3-2. I had a bit of a chat to the guy next to me who was a Bradford exile living in Cheltenham, "they look like a work in progress to me" he said. Well I don't think that work has finished yet. I then drove home in the dark and inevitably 3 junctions of the M5 were closed. Home by 1 am.

Salford

What to say about Salford? An interesting location for a football ground. Right in the middle of a Jewish community, many of whom are so strict in their observance of their sabbath that they wont even touch a mobile phone on that day, and certainly wouldn't go to a game. I know this from first hand experience as on the way to a ground we got stopped by a distressed young lady who needed to call an ambulance for her ailing father but needed me to make the call as she couldn't touch the phone. I thought this was some elaborate con trick, but it all checked out and the ambulance turned up.

So, apart from being a Gary Neville vanity project what can I say? There is a nice quirky pub "The Star Inn" community run which welcomes away fans and it's a nice walk from there to the ground. It is also easy to park by the Star so don't go near the ground or you will get a parking ticket. Much to the annoyance of Gary, despite being the big budget club every season they have failed to make headway for several years now and seem stuck in league 2. Still, I suppose Gary can afford this. Who knows where they are heading with this "project", but it makes an easy away game for me to get to.

Salford's nickname is the "ammies", apparently from when they were amateur in the 60's. You would think they might change that? Other clubs change their nickname on a regular basis and the memories are soon forgotten. Ask a Reading fan for instance, who the biscuitmen are and it is very likely that they will be surprised to find it is their own club. I have never heard any Bradford fan call us the Paraders. We are the bantams (for now?).

Tranmere Again and again and again

In 2014, I found myself sitting next to Peter Johnson, the then owner of Tranmere Rovers. And what a lovely chap he was, quite delightful company. My mate Alan (remember him, the one who suggested the night out at Anfield in 1984?) had been invited for a look around the Large Hadron Collider at CERN in Geneva. Apparently this was not the sort of thing that appealed to Alans wife, but the chance to geek out to some big physics appealed to me, so off we went. The whole event was a totally transparent attempt by my old university to beg some charitable donations. A less deserving cause than a modern University is hard to think of, so they weren't getting any money out of me or Alan. Alan got invited (I think) because his job title was Technical Director at Rolls Royce. I think they thought he was THE technical Director, not just one of many.

There is no doubt Alan has made a success of his life. He is Director of a major Research Institute now. He got one "O" Level. He is the only person I know who resat their O Levels. It seems to have done him the world of good. It just goes to show that a little failure can spur you on to success.

Anyway. I'm eating my free meal and chatting away to Peter. Top bloke as I say and of course we are talking football. Peter is well known to be a Liverpool fan, but when Everton were struggling for cash in the mid 90's he helped out. This did not go down well with the Everton fans. You can't help some people. Peter told me that one day during this period he was getting a black cab from Lime Street up to Everton. The taxi driver recognised him and said, "You're that Peter Johnson aren't you?". Peter agreed. At that point the cab driver got out of his car and bellowed to all his mates "Hey lads, Adolf Hitler,

Margaret Thatcher, and now Peter Johnson" I've had the full set now!", and then got back in and drove him to Goodison.

So I've always had a bit of a soft spot for Tranmere. For the last three seasons Bradford have been drawn to play Tranmere in the league, away on a Tuesday night. Its less than an hour away for me so you can't say no. The first year we drove past the ground to The Cock and Bottle, an OK choice but not quite right. The next time we tried a pub before the ground (The Travellers Rest), conveniently located on the main road from the motorway to the ground and perfectly pleasant with nice beer, but still not quite right. So this last time we tried the Fan Park. In general, I steer clear of fan parks. It's usually an opportunity to buy overpriced plastic bottles of Heineken. But I'd read good things. It didn't disappoint. Although they had plastic glasses everything else was up to scratch. 5 or 6 different choices of beers and some gorgeous pies. And friendly fans. They told me all away fans apart from Bolton and Wrexham have been welcome. At present the fan park is housed in a huge temporary marquee. But behind this is the frame for a huge wooden building. Well done Tranmere. More clubs should do this – especially the soulless out of town mob.

There was also football. All three games finished 2-1 and we won one of them. The last game turned out to be Mark Hughes last game as Bradford manager. He was average. Bradfords problems run deeper than the manager so I doubt I will look back on this as a turning point.

Carlisle

I will be honest up front. I haven't enjoyed my two trips to Carlisle. Maybe if you are a Carlisle fan, as a home fan you see this as a good thing? Anyway, where I live I have two options. A car drive for 2 hours straight up the M6 or a train journey up the west coast mainline straight into Carlisle.

The first time, we drove. The ground is on the main road between the town centre and the motorway so if you drive you are left with the option of driving past the ground (not great in the congestion after a match) or sticking with the pubs on the motorway side of the ground. So that's what we did. These pubs are either chain pubs or even worse, hotel bars. Not what I'm looking for at all.

So the second time, we went by train. This didn't work either. The train itself was fine for once but we couldn't get in a pub! It was the play off semifinal second leg so for some unknown reason, none of the pubs would let Under 18s in. Even Wetherspoons. How does this help with policing? The only pub in the whole town centre that would let us in was Brewdog. So, for once, thanks Brewdog. I used to love Brewdog when they were the "plucky little minnows" taking on the big boys. But I really feel they have grown too big for their boots now. Anyway, they did us proud.

I don't like the ground either. For me, the away fans should be stood behind the goal. There is a perfectly serviceable away terrace, open air but that's fine by me. I am happy to bring a coat with a hood to a winter game. It feels authentic. The first time we went this stand was closed so we had to sit at the side. Not good. The second time it was full of home fans (sellout crowd) so again, not good. Maybe I will have a better time when Eddie turns 18? At least we can all have a beer in a hopefully nice pub.

Forest Green

For me Forest Green wins the prize for being the most bizarre, unique, unlikely, unfeasible location for a football league ground. My son Sam was at Birmingham University so Tom and I travelled down to Birmingham to pick him up and head off into the Cotswolds. We had done our research so headed off to the George Inn, a nice enough country pub outside Nailsworth. Have you heard of Nailsworth? Because it's the largest village anywhere near Forest Green. We are drinking beer and staring at the countryside. Google maps tells us it's a 15 minute walk to the New Lawn stadium so it must be right.

We set off for the ground up a footpath behind the pub and after 5 minutes uphill find ourselves in a council estate. Not very Cotswolds. Five minutes through the estate and you are on the one road in and out of the New Lawn to the "vast metropolis" of Nailsworth. The traffic is chaos and it's not even a big crowd. We had already been prepared that Forest Green are a "vegan" team so there would be no meat pies. But there were some very unhappy Bradford fans when we got in the away end. There is a rule that you can't sell alcohol in view of the pitch and there was nowhere else to put the kiosk, so no beer. We had a vegan roll and felt happy that we had already had our beer.

Bradford had been pretty poor this season and Forest Green were top so it was a bit of a surprise to be leading 1-0 coming into the closing stage of the game. Forest Green get one final corner and throw everything forward. The corner comes in and the ball breaks loose. Unbelievably Andy Cook, not known for his speed over any distance, outsprints everyone and takes the ball up the other end to seal the game 2-0. "I'm goosed" he said, when he finally got enough breath back to speak. So we leave FGR by the only single track road available and there is an old guy from FGR thanking us for attending the game and congratulating us on the result. I haven't seen that anywhere else.

FGR is essentially a vanity project by the owner Dale Vince and you have to feel that he could get bored at any point and the club would then just disappear like others have before. That said, Dale has ambitious plans to relocate the club closer to the M5 and build a unique stadium out of wood. As a Bradford fan I feel queasy just thinking about a wooden stadium, but the experts say it will be safe. We shall see. At time of writing FGR are back in Division 2 and very near the bottom, it will be interesting to see if Dale invests in the transfer window.

Northampton

If there is one fixture that sums up the life changes between the carefree youth who started the quest to visit the 92 and the care worn middle aged man who is finally finishing it off, it is Northampton.

I first visited Northampton on a whim on 20th February 1990. I had started a job in Solihull a week earlier and so found myself in a strange town with no friends nearby. I was frankly bored. It was a Tuesday night so there must be some football on. A quick check on teletext showed that the nearest game was Northampton vs Walsall. About an hour's drive – that will do me. I head off towards the M6, that's where Northampton is right? No sat nav in those days. Heading M6 and then south on the M1 there's a sign for Northampton and at that stage I realise I haven't got a clue where I'm going and I can't see any tell-tale floodlights anywhere.

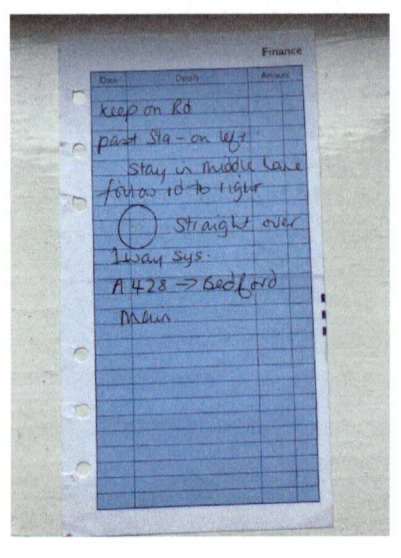

Maybe Northampton is bigger than just a football ground? So I stop at the next garage, top up the car with a bit of petrol and wander in to pay, but really to ask for some directions. A lady next to me in the queue hears my question and immediately tears a page from her Filofax (ah the 90's!) and scrawls some directions down to hand to me. I still have these directions, 33 years later, tucked away in the match programme. I must have looked confused (Keep on rd, past sta on left, stay mid lane, follow rd to right etc) so she says, "No worries, I'm going that way, follow me". Even better, so we head of to our cars and I discover I have just met the 1990 equivalent of Lewis Hamilton, fortunately I am no slouch either and we tear across the Northampton suburbs at breakneck speed. Eventually the warm glow of the floodlights appear and she gives me a cheery wave goodbye – Thank you, whoever you were.

If Carlsberg did away games…. My first visit to Sixfields, the new Northampton "abomination" wouldn't be far off the mark for me. Pretty much the perfect away day experience.

Thirty three years later and it's the "squeaky bum" end of the season. Bradford have a reasonable chance of the play offs and an outside chance of automatics. Away at Northampton, who are currently in third, the last automatic place. Clearly this is a game not to be missed. I have looked at Northampton may times over the years since they moved ground, with really no excitement to visit. Three miles out of town, no pubs, Cineworld, Argos and Wickes with a TGI Friday really not my thing at all. But this is going to have to be done, so the military planning begins. Country pubs en-route are considered and discarded and after much agonising I plump for the "Malt Shovel Tavern".

 I could not have chosen better. Not only is this a real proper old school pub with 8 real ales on hand pump. It happens to be having a free beer festival with a further 50 beers and a barbeque in the beer garden. Absolute heaven. You can see a few of the extra barrels behind us.

It's late April and it's also a beautiful sunny day, surely the day couldn't get any better. I often think, when I hit the 2 pint happy place that I shouldn't go to the game as it will just ruin my mood, but I always go. As it turns out much excitement remained. Firstly, Tony had obviously enjoyed the beer as well. As we walked back to the car there were a lot of pro-lifers campaigning against abortion. Unusually for Tony, he wound down the window as we drove past and gave them a fruity discourse as to his alternate views on the subject. I'm sure that told them!

My military planning had identified a range of parking options by the ground and we end up in a field. Perfect on a sun-drenched April day but I wonder what it's like on a wet February evening? The game goes to plan, Northampton play the better football and Bradford take the lead. Eventually Northampton equalise and batter us for the remainder of the game. A win would see them promoted. Into injury time and Bradford break and score. Heartbreak for the Northampton fans and they stream out of the stadium in their masses. They should not worry. They will go up winning away at Tranmere the following week.

In truth, this new ground is as much a horror as the other new grounds I've visited but it's worth making the effort to combine with the town centre.

Colchester, Sutton and Crawley

Now these are the games that I had really been avoiding on the grounds that they really are a long way from where I live and there really is a good chance that if I wait long enough they won't be in the league any more. But there comes a time. That time turned out to be my youngest son getting a taste for a road trip and a long car journey to an away ground.

My mate Lee (Newcastle fan) confided in me that the only conversation he had with his dad through his entire teenage years was football. It's a good job, football existed he said, or we would have said nowt to each other for 10 years. Lee was a big magpies fan and he pulled off a nice little trick in naming his first son. His wife said "I like Robert" as a name. Quick as a flash Lee replied. "That's nice and we could give him my name Lee as his middle name". So he got to call his first born Robert Lee. No, not the confederate general, the Newcastle Utd midfielder. I wonder if his wife ever found out? They are now divorced.

Anyway, no Dad should be turning down a chance to bond with his son over 8 hours in a car on a Saturday afternoon. So away we went. Down the M6, through the interminable miles of Staffordshire, along the toll road and then sat nav kicks in to guide you to the ground of the day. All to the tunes of Spotify and a chance to educate my son to the best songs from the 70's, 80's and occasionally 90's.

Colchester was first up. An out of town monstrosity. So a long walk to a pub. The fanzone is classic plastic bottled Heineken. So was the game! Our season was over so we had decided to put the reserves out to see how they played. And they played badly! Colchester won't have had an easier 3-0 win all season. Oh well, lesson learned and we had a very nice time together. So much so that next month Sutton could not be resisted.

If Sutton was non-league it would be a great ground, in a proper area with pubs and even a nice park for a walk to the ground. But let's be honest it's not really up to league status is it. Its tiny, there aren't any pies for sale in the ground (criminal) and when I went to collect the tickets they are just a print out on an A4 piece of paper. Although, to be fair, it was a yellow piece of paper. And green if you were in the seats! We won 4-1 and this was such fun we had to do this again. So where next? Crawley!

I quite liked Crawley, if you are prepared to put a bit of a walk in, it's got a lovely town centre and some nice pubs. I recommend the Brewery Shades. The ground is a bit of an out of town monstrosity, but I've been to worse. It's very close to the M23 for a quick getaway so that's nice and there is plenty of free parking in the nearby housing estates. But there are subways around the ground to get back to the car. I have never liked a subway. Are we designing a natural ambush point? I suppose Crawley is a fairly safe place. But anyway, when we were at the game it rained and on the way back the underpass was "flooded" with about 2 inches of rainwater. There were huge crowds refusing to walk through this, Eddie and I barged past and splashed through. I've seen bigger floods in the toilets at Swansea.

Barrow and Harrogate

There was a time when you didn't need to worry about whether you would get a ticket for a Bradford game. Now, the smaller and closer away games all sell out. Coming towards the end of my 92 I was particularly worried about these two. In the 21/22 season I had declined the opportunity to visit Barrow and Harrogate for very different reasons. Barrow was a Xmas game and I was already down to visit 3 games at Xmas so in the spirit of domestic harmony I declined that one. Bad decision as it happens as two of the other three games were called off for bad weather and Bradford won at Barrow. Oh well, you lose some, and you lose some more.

Harrogate (Feb 22) was and remains the only game I have ever really wanted to go to that I have failed to get a ticket. Think about that, I even got a ticket for the England Euros final, two FA Cup finals and 2 league cup finals, but not Harrogate away. The maximum allocation in the away end is 850 and Bradford had plenty more "away priority members" than that. By the time the freebies and sponsors have had their share who knows how many actually go on sale. The best way to get a ticket is to go to the ticket office and queue, but that's not really practical as I was 60 miles away, it's a weekday and I have a job. So I go to the online queue at 9 am and am unsurprised to fail to get a ticket. Not to be perturbed I call up Harrogate to ask about executive packages. Apparently the normal prawn sandwich tickets are all sold out but they are doing an extra allocation. "One Course meal (?) and half a bottle of wine at the local Cresta Court hotel and then walked to your seat. £45 (I think). Tony is not keen and says he will wait until next year as we really aren't going up. I'm not keen to go as nobby no mates and sit and pretend not to be a Bradford fan, presumably with quite a lot more Bradford fans, so I regretfully leave it.

So in the 22/23 season there was a lot of pressure to get tickets. I enquired at the very start of the season about prawn sandwich tickets at Harrogate but they were all gone. (I'm guessing Cresta Court didn't run smoothly?). Anyhow we were on our new away ticket scheme this season with loyalty points where fans who have a season ticket and have been to the most away games get first dibs, so no-one knew how this would turn out.

Barrow was our first away game of the season and hopes would still be high for a good season so tickets would be hard to get.

As it turned out, possibly because a lot of people are still on holiday on 6th August (including Tony) I got two tickets, so Eddie and I were good to go. We headed off up the M6 and through the beautiful countryside to the not so beautiful town of Barrow at the end of the Cumbria peninsular. We parked up near the ground and headed off to find a pub. Walking down the main road there was a huge police presence for two hours before the game. Pretty much next door was an equally huge "gang" of teenage lads all clad in Stone Island and CP company and shouting random abuse at anyone walking past. Welcome to Barrow. We escaped down to town and found a good enough pub opposite a statue of Emlyn Hughes. I did not know he was a local lad. Back up to the ground for 2.30 and the teenagers had dispersed.

Barrow is not an impressive ground, even by non-league standards. The away terrace is in the corner. First panic was, where are the pies. Fortunately the kiosk was hidden behind a screen, to allow fans to have a beer. So pie panic over. But then the next question is, where are you going to stand?. There are barely any steps and there was also a random block of concrete. Several people tried to stand on this and got told to get off as they were blocking the view for everyone else. I'm really not sure how they got a safety certificate. I won't be rushing back. You can see from the picture below just how impressive the away end is.

Harrogate was also early season, but being 1st October no one would be away on holiday and being a very short local bus ride away from Bradford, a lot of people would want to go. I was really worried we would miss out so I was monitoring the social media feeds hourly to check if the tickets were on sale. If you are a staunch monarchist you might want to skip the rest of this paragraph. I think we had a stroke of luck in that the Queen died on the 8th September just as the tickets were about to go on sale. The club must have not wanted to do any social media at such a sombre time so the tickets went on sale with no social media announcement at all. But we were watching. So I nipped in quickly and got tickets for Me, Eddie and Tony. It was on!

The game was an early kick off on the Saturday. I always regard this as a pain as it doesn't suit the pre-match pub ritual. We found an ok pub near the ground but I'm sure Harrogate has better offerings further into town. Another day. Harrogate is a genteel place compared to Bradford and also well heeled. Nothing exemplified this more that the pie option. "Artisanal pies", no Pukka here! Delicious but pricey and tiny. After this tasty morsel Tony decided this definitely wasn't enough and disappeared. He came back with three trays packed full of pie, peas, potatoes, gravy etc. A full on meal. God knows how much he spent!

Milton Keynes

I've checked my records and have confirmed that up until Tuesday 24th October 2023 I had never seen MK Dons play. When I tell people the diminishing list of grounds I have left to do they often assume I am boycotting MK Dons in solidarity with Wimbledon. This would be a worthy story but it's not true. It's just not happened for me. Family holidays and end of season apathy have combined to mean I have never bothered to go. Checking on the excellent 11v11 website this means I have missed 16 chances (home and away) to see MK Dons. Until now.

If you have ever been to Milton Keynes you will know it is an unusual place, all horizontal and vertical avenues, roundabouts and occasional glimpses of life going on, followed by a field. So it needs a little planning. Here's how to "do" MK Dons. Aim to arrive early if it's going to be busy. Set the satnav for the ground and as you get to the lights to turn into the ground turn right into the industrial estate opposite. Do not turn left into the land of TGI Friday and Next outlets. You will pay £7 for the privilege of sitting in a big queue after the game. There is loads of free parking in the industrial estate opposite. Walk to Bletchley. It's a mile and a bit. The walk presents the full gamut of the Milton Keynes experience, dual carriageway, underpass, shops,

Marshall Amps headquarters, even the odd country house and old village high street. Bletchley has a Wetherspoons. "The Captain Ridley's Shooting Party". I always think that if the CAMRA good beer guide lists a Wetherspoons then it is a place struggling for a decent pub. Don't get me wrong. I love Wetherspoons as an institution. £2.48 for a pint of good quality real ale in October 23 is a bargain. I just don't want my memories of away grounds to all be of Wetherspoons. This one is dedicated to the code breakers of course, with a picture of Alan Turing, some old WW2 memorabilia and an enigma machine in a glass cabinet. I'm guessing it's your best bet unless you like overpriced lager in the stadium or the TGI Fridays by the ground. A leisurely couple of pints then walk back to the ground. If you are short of time the 'Spoons has a car park and you can drive back and probably still get parked up if it's not a busy night.

As you can see, this is a big stadium to fill. This was not a busy night. 5,500 people in a stadium designed for over 30,000. Lovely padded seats mind. I'm surprised that even that many go. "It's football Jim but not as we know it". If they had an 8,000 capacity ground maybe it would have had some character but this just feels like a reserve team game.

Wrexham

A quick trip down the M56 from Warrington and one I would not be making if I didn't need a tick on my list. Bradford are awful, currently 8 league games without a win. There is seemingly not a lot of hope for us versus a Ryan Reynolds supercharged Wrexham. We all love him 'til its our club. Ah well, travel in hope.

Still, the day starts well. I have spotted The Magic Dragon Brewery Tap in the beer guide. Five of its own ales on hand pull and guess what – its Welsh Language Music Day which is a couple of middle age ladies belting out Adele and Abba in Welsh and in fine voice. All really jolly. So much so that we stay for an extra half, but then someone starts singing that awful Wrexham song from the Disney series and it's time to make our way to the ground.

It's a pretty decent ground and in usual style we are allocated seat numbers that nobody pays attention to and we stand where we like. If you paid really close attention I didn't say who I went to the Everton game with, back in the 90's. This is because I have totally forgotten the guys name. But today I think I have found him, so during a lull in play I ask him if he used to live in Chippenham in the 90's and he looks at me quite suspiciously. I'm just trying to find the guy I used to go to the odd game with I explain, and it turns out his wife is from Chippenham! What a small world. The hunt for my Chippenham man continues.

The game continues and for 80 minutes Bradford are resolute in defence without really offering anything upfront. Finally we venture forward and are awarded a penalty. "Please don't let Cook take it" we plead. He has been awful on penalties this season. Sure enough he takes it and sure enough he fires it straight at the keeper for an easy save.

And that you would think would be that, but it strangely seems to galvanise Bradford and we start attacking. I have no belief so I wander off for my old man's large prostate pre drive home toilet trip. Just as I am passing Charlie on my way back to the seats we attack, we shoot, it is saved and Cook with the determination of a man possessed bundles the ball over the line. Scenes!, Huge hugs with Charlie and some random guy and then back to my own seats for a second round of huge hugs with Eddie and Tony.

The ref of course insists on finding 8 minutes of injury time from somewhere and we have to endure several spirited Tozer long throws, but eventually it's done, a smash and grab? But the first team in over 2 years to stop Wrexham scoring at home – so huge credit to the lads.

Southampton

18th April 2024. I have decided to get the last four grounds done. I can always come back and see them again should Bradford perk up or we get lucky with a cup draw. My mate Dave (Stoke fan) has managed to navigate the byzantine bureaucracy of getting two tickets behind the goal in the away end for Southampton vs Stoke. I surprise myself that I am inordinately excited by the prospect of this trip. I wonder why?

It's that stage of the season when the "statto" in us gets excited working out the permutations for promotion and relegation. Southampton have put together a late surge and are now unlikely gate crashers into the automatic promotion slots. They are 3 points behind Leeds with a game in hand and 4 points behind Leicester. Win away at Cardiff and away at Leicester and they will be at least second. Equally Stoke need a win to pull themselves out of the relegation mire. So the game could be a dead rubber or could be absolutely vital for one or both teams. The joy of the end of season. It could be I am excited because I have a chance to see Leeds fall apart again by Southampton nicking second place off them. But actually I think it is because I can now smell the finishing line on my quest for the 92. With Southampton off the list I will only have 3 left to do and with Bolton within cycling distance of my house I really only have two challenges remaining. Luton and Sunderland. Which one for the grand finale?

Anyway, out comes the beer guide and the Guide Dog is selected. 10 cask ales on hand pump and apparently a great atmosphere on match day. A 22 minute walk to the ground so far enough away to avoid the more "lively" element of the Stoke and Southampton fans[4]. Let's do this.

Of course, by the day of the game Stoke have won and Southampton have lost twice so it is a pretty dead rubber. Southampton secure in the play offs with no hope of automatic promotion and Stoke pretty much secure in the championship for another season.

Dave is worried about the traffic so we set off early (8 am) and by 11 we are less than an hour from the ground so we stop at a costa coffee on the A34. Blimey, fast food and the UK! It takes us nearly 20 minutes to get served! 2 minimum wage staff struggling to make iced frappa latte chinos or whatever god awful stuff it is they sell. Replete with coffee we head back onto the road and are on Earls road by the pub just after 12. It turns out this is a decent spot as this is right on the boundary of the

---

[4] If you are lucky enough to get to see your team at Wembley you will be allocated a pub. If this is "The Green Man" don't go unless you are after a bunch of "hoodie boys" screaming and spraying beer all over the place. If you want a beer go to the Wetherspoons a mile away.

residents only parking zone so we park up for free[5] – always a bonus.

Into the pub and one hard stare from a local who obviously suspects we have dodgy allegiance but it's a nice pub and a very nice pint or two of Thornbridge Jaipur. I chat to the locals wishing them the best of luck beating Leeds in the play offs – then it's off to the ground. Quite without knowing it, Dave has bought us safe standing tickets. You can see my comments on safe standing in the Derby section, but suffice to say we would have stood all game anyway. Southampton play some good football for the first 10-20 minutes but you can see their heart is not in it. Slowly Stoke get into the game and score a decent goal. A win is absolute guaranteed safety, but the jubilation is not "off the scale". I think the fans sense they are safe anyway and are just a bit sad to be even close to relegation when they believe they should be much higher up the table. (I know that feeling!). Samuel Edozie and Kyle Walker Peters combine to cause a fair few problems on the right wing but the rest of the Saints look disinterested. In the second half the ref ignores a stone wall penalty for Stoke but it matters not. The whistle goes and Stoke are safe. Job done for my mate Dave.

Out of the ground and Dave is amazed the away fans are allowed to mingle with the home fans – "They usually keep us in" – really? I must have been in the lower leagues for too long! Anyway, absolutely no bother with the locals on the way back to the car and we hatch a plan. Neither of us is in a rush to get home and I have noticed that Tamworth is essentially on the route home. Tamworth being home to the "Tamworth Tap". Currently CAMRA pub of the year. I set the satnav for Tamworth, 2.5 hours – that's OK and off we go.

---

[5] Note to younger readers – it is a true sign of middle age when your concern switches from getting tickets to the gig to getting a good parking space!

I did all the driving down to Southampton so Dave offered to drive us to Tamworth, "Right just make sure we don't miss the turning for the A34 and it is straight there!........

Of course, we get chatting and obviously miss the turning off the M3 for the A34. "Bollocks" we cry in unison as we realise a second too late what we have done. "This route is 45 minutes longer" chirps the sat nav helpfully. Fortunately we spot a triangular route back to the A34 and it ends up costing us 15 minutes – oh well, not too bad.

We arrive in Tamwoth just after 8 and it seems a pleasant enough place. Nice car park free after 6 pm, and make our way to the pub. We wander up to the Tamworth tap and there's a bunch of middle age people having a chat and pretty much blocking the door. In my usual manner I brush through and as I get to the door a matronly woman says "That's ok we have had a few people leave, there is room for you". So in we go, the place is reasonably busy, but certainly not crushed. I get us a couple of pints and we sit down by the window and watch as the same matronly women turn away 3 lads in their 20's. There is plenty of room in the pub and the lads really didn't look like trouble. Has fame gone to their heads? Or does Tamwoth have a seedy Saturday night? Anyway, the pub itself and the beer is ok. But I would be voting for the Black Country Arms ahead of it!

Back to the car and home. Just over 450 miles, so our unplanned diversion and our pitstop in Tamwoth together have cost us 20 miles – not too bad. On the last leg with about 10 miles to go an orange "idiot light" pings on[6]. What the hell, we are nearly home – so I drive on and everything is fine. As I drop Dave off at 10-30

---

[6] I look it up in the manual next day (Oh, alright I admit, I used YouTube) and it is a blown full beam bulb. I tell Eddie I will fix it and he laughs "You can't do that Dad!" – what a role model I am. So I spring into action and fix it. There! That will show him! -

he notes. "Well I am not doing Luton or Bolton, but I am up for Sunderland". Great – now I just need next seasons fixture list.

One final post script which will take us nicely to Luton. Ir is becoming increasingly difficult, if not impossible to attend a game without being a "registered fan" of one of the two teams playing. At a very minimum this is a right pain in the arse for those of us who like to ground hop. Here is my ticket for Southampton:

I am registered as Mr "Away Supporter". We managed to confound the system on this occasion but I shouldn't have to be a registered stoke fan just to go see them play.

Southampton joins the list. 118 league grounds, 102 different clubs and 95 different clubs I have seen Bradford play at. I have 3 clubs left to do to get the current 92. I am left hoping for a good cup draw. Or a promotion. Preferably both.

The Never Ending Story

This book was written from the perspective of the 2023/24 season. I will continue to update it as I crawl closer to the final destination, beyond this chapter lie the additions made after Southampton.

A little research reveals that (correct in 23/24 season) to do the 92 "my way", that is to say by visiting all 92 clubs with your own team you currently have to be a fan of one of five clubs:

Bradford, Swindon and Notts County all of whom you would have needed to start watching in the 1990's.

Northampton – a tougher ask as you would have had to start watching in 1965, but feasible if you are say 70 plus.

Port Vale – a really tough ask. You would have needed to have started in 1929. Let me know if you are out there!

For those of you that like lists here is what I still have to do. It is the unlikely mix of Sunderland, Luton and Bolton. I will try to make an "event" of some kind at the last one. Then (and in parallel) my attention will turn to the clubs I have not seen Bradford play at: West Ham, Blackpool, Newcastle, Southampton and Sheffield Wednesday. I may also visit Crystal Palace which has become an oddity on my list. I have been to Crystal Palace twice. Once to see Palace play QPR, and once for Wimbledon vs Bradford. So I can't decide if I need to go back. It is a long way, but let's be honest. I will go if the chance arises!

Finally there will be the new grounds and the new entries from non-league. It will never end, but I feel the bulk is done now. Driving home from MK Dons with Eddie, he said, "I don't want to do the 92". I am an inspiration!

APPENDIX

The "Missing" Teams

Luton

Immediate apologies to the good folk and fans of Luton. I really don't like Luton. This is not down to the fans, it is down to a certain Mr David Evans (google him). My dislike for Luton started on a cold winters evening back in 1987 (I think). We were all set for a midweek game at Anfield. A little snow was forecast so we were all hoping for the orange ball. Wrap up warm and enjoy the fun. We arrived at the ground, The Luton fans arrived at the ground (having come on the National Express coach). But the Luton team never came. It later emerged that they had seen the forecast and decided it was too dangerous to travel. But of course, didn't get permission to cancel the game or tell the fans. The pies were given out to the homeless and Luton were fined. But not an auspicious start to my relationship with Luton.

Enter Mr David Evans MP. Tory MP and chairman of Luton Town. It is fair to say he had a right hump on about hooligans as he was chairman of Luton in March 1985 when Millwall rioted and caused a lot of damage. His solution was to ban away fans (This is anathema to everything I hold sacred). Luton in fact went further. Evans not only banned away fans, they introduced identity cards for home fans, despite criticism from the football league. The league did insist that Luton allow away fans for cup matches and when Luton refused they were thrown out of the League Cup. After this admonishment Luton did relent and allow away fans for cup ties only. The scheme lasted for four seasons.

They also installed an awful plastic pitch. Today, modern 4G pitches are excellent, but still not allowed above non league level in England. They were nowhere near good enough in the 1980's.

A final word on Evans, according to Wikipedia "Shortly before losing his seat, in early March 1997, he attracted controversy over unguarded remarks in an interview by sixth-formers at Stanborough School for a school magazine in which he referred to his opponent Melanie Johnson as a "single girl" (she was 42 years old at the time) with "bastard children" and claimed that the Birmingham Six were guilty and had "killed hundreds" before being caught, as well as making remarks considered racist, such as asking how the sixth-formers would feel if their daughter was raped by "some black bastard". – Lovely Chap!

Bolton

Bolton is a strange one for me. I live so close by I really should have been. But I have always assumed that I would get a Bradford game so have never just ticked it off my list. Let's look at the Bolton vs Bradford chances I have missed:

27th October 2020 – No fans allowed – COVID
5th September 2020– No fans allowed – COVID
3rd September 2019 – football league trophy – couldn't be bothered – surely I will get a proper game not this mickey mouse trophy
24th September 2016 – Away in Isle of Man on a pre booked (before fixture list announced) sportive, cycling the IOM TT circuit
26th December 1998 – Boxing day and in the first flush of romance with my now wife, Not happening!
1st January 1997 – New years day, At home in Swindon with flu
19th December 1992, 11th April 1992, 7th December 91, 1st September 90 – living in Solihull, not really, there is always another chance, right?
6th May 1985 – Blimey - I have only just started going to games and I have no car, this one will have to wait.

So, I have had my half chances over the years but it may well never happen now. We will see.

Sunderland

It is not that surprising that I have not ticked Sunderland off my list (yet!). Whilst Bradford played Sunderland regularly in the 80's and more sporadically from 1990 to 2003, I was always living at least three hours drive from the game. There was a lot of much more attractive lower hanging fruit to go at, Sunderland could wait. From 2003 onwards there has only been two chances to see the Stadium of Light. One was a league game in December 2018 when I was on holiday skiing in Canade (oooh, ark at me!). The only other was a Football League Trophy game on a cold Tuesday night in November 2021. I did ask Tom and Tony but unsurprisingly they weren't up for it. In retrospect I should have gone.

Appendix 2 – Grounds Visited

League teams Visited with Bradford		
Home Team	Date	Away team
Bradford C	29/12/1984	Bolton
Huddersfield	07/09/1985	Bradford
Reading	11/04/1987	Bradford
Derby	20/04/1987	Bradford
Shrewsbury	26/09/1987	Bradford
Barnsley	07/11/1987	Bradford
Leeds	01/01/1988	Bradford
Birmingham	05/03/1988	Bradford
Aston Villa	02/05/1988	Bradford
Man C	10/12/1988	Bradford
Hull	26/12/1988	Bradford
Stoke	14/01/1989	Bradford
West Brom	20/09/1989	Bradford
Blackburn R	01/01/1990	Bradford
Middlesboro	16/04/1990	Bradford
Bournemouth	18/09/1990	Bradford
Crewe	27/10/1990	Bradford
Tranmere	18/01/1991	Bradford
Crystal Palace	16/02/1991	QPR
Preston	23/02/1991	Bradford
Cambridge	07/05/1991	Bradford
Wigan	11/01/1992	Bradford
Fulham	02/05/1992	Bradford
Plymouth	22/08/1992	Bradford
Mansfield	12/09/1992	Bradford

Swansea	26/09/1992	Bradford
Brighton	27/01/1993	Bradford
Exeter	03/04/1993	Bradford
Port Vale	13/04/1993	Bradford
Leyton Orient	01/05/1993	Bradford
Bristol R	09/10/1993	Bradford
Burnley	15/01/1994	Bradford
Peterboro	14/01/1995	Bradford
Brentford	11/02/1995	Bradford
Oxford	18/03/1995	Bradford
Cardiff	28/03/1995	Bradford
Wycombe	04/04/1995	Bradford
Notts C	29/08/1995	Bradford
Swindon	13/09/1995	Bradford
Notts F	04/10/1995	Bradford
Chesterfield	04/11/1995	Bradford
Rotherham	23/01/1996	Bradford
Bristol C	24/02/1996	Bradford
Sheff Utd	10/09/1996	Bradford
QPR	16/10/1996	Bradford
Charlton	23/11/1996	Bradford
Grimsby	21/12/1996	Bradford
Everton	25/01/1997	Bradford
Stockport	10/01/1998	Bradford
Ipswich	31/01/1998	Bradford
Norwich	04/04/1998	Bradford
Watford	15/08/1998	Bradford
Lincoln	18/08/1998	Bradford
Wolves	09/05/1999	Bradford
Liverpool	01/11/1999	Bradford

Tottenham	04/03/2000	Bradford
Man U	05/09/2000	Bradford
Arsenal	30/01/2001	Bradford
Coventry	19/05/2001	Bradford
Leicester	17/09/2002	Bradford
Walsall	06/12/2003	Bradford
Doncaster	24/03/2005	Bradford
Accrington	11/10/2008	Bradford
Chelsea	24/01/2015	Bradford
Fleetwood	12/09/2015	Bradford
Burton	06/02/2016	Bradford
Millwall	20/05/2016	Bradford
Wimbledon	29/10/2016	Bradford
Portsmouth	28/10/2017	Bradford
Gillingham	27/10/2018	Bradford
Cheltenham	17/09/2019	Bradford
Morecambe	11/10/2019	Bradford
Newport	22/02/2020	Bradford
Salford	07/03/2020	Bradford
Carlisle	08/01/2022	Bradford
Stevenage	08/02/2022	Bradford
Colchester	18/04/2022	Bradford
Barrow	06/08/2022	Bradford
Harrogate	01/10/2022	Bradford
Crawley	07/04/2023	Bradford
Northampton	29/04/2023	Bradford
MK Dons	24/10/2023	Bradford
Wrexham	10/02/2024	Bradford

Note – Crystal Palace also visited when Wimbledon played Bradford.

League teams Visited - no Bradford		
Home Team	Date	Away team
W. Ham	20/05/1985	Liverpool
Sheff W	29/03/1986	Liverpool
Blackpool	24/10/1987	Wigan
Newcastle	04/02/1989	Liverpool
Southampton	27/04/2024	Stoke

Non league visited whilst in league		
Bury	29/02/1992	Bradford
Chester	13/08/1994	Bradford
Halifax	02/12/1988	Crewe
Hereford	27/03/1993	Bury
Rochdale	10/03/2009	Bradford
York	29/01/1994	Bradford
Yeovil	06/01/2018	Bradford
Macclesfield	02/02/2008	Bradford
Southend	12/04/1997	Bradford
Oldham	31/10/1989	Bradford
Scunthorpe	22/11/1988	Bradford
Hartlepool	26/12/1991	Bradford
Sutton Utd	22/04/2022	Bradford
Forest Green	12/03/2022	Bradford

Second grounds visited		
Listed as new ground unless never saw City at old ground		
Bradford (odsal)	20/09/1986	Leeds
Huddersfield (McAlpine)	12/08/1997	Bradford
Stoke (Awful new thing)	16/01/1998	Bradford

Derby (Awful new thing)	15/03/2003	Bradford
Reading (Awful new thing)	16/03/2015	Bradford
Wigan (DW)	19/03/2016	Bradford
Rotherham (Awful new thing)	23/01/2018	Bradford
Shrewsbury (Awful new thing)	04/08/2018	Bradford
Bristol Rovers (Memorial)	02/04/2022	Bradford
Wimbledon (Plough Lane)	14/01/2023	Bradford
Doncaster (Awful new thing)	25/02/2023	Bradford
Leicester (Filbert Street)	30/04/1986	Liverpool
Walsall (Fellows Park)	12/10/1988	Liverpool
Chester (Sealand Road)	10/09/1989	Bristol C
Millwall (Old Den)	19/09/1989	Liverpool
Northampton (County Ground)	20/02/1990	Walsall

Acknowledgements

I would like to thank Pat, Tony and Klaas, for their help in proof reading, for jogging my memory with extra snippets I had completely forgotten and most of all for their most excellent company on this life long journey I have chosen.

I also wish to thank the many people who have accompanied me over the years at these games. My three sons who often come and 2 are season ticket holders, my wife who put up with a few games in the early days but is most honourably mentioned for encouraging me to go to Chelsea, and also my friends who are not Bradford fans but who came in the away end with me anyway.

I would also like to Thank Rob (Reading fan) for staying away from Valley Parade. Without fail every time he comes with us we lose. The only exception being the time he came to the pub with us and then sat with the Reading fans. We drew 0-0. Thanks Rob.

And finally, thanks to Dave with help sorting the front cover and all the publishing minutiae.

Printed in Great Britain
by Amazon